HAUNTINGS
IN YORKSHIRE

Real life tales from the Ridings

Stephen Wade

HALSGROVE

First published in Great Britain by Halsgrove, 2008
Reprinted 2018

Copyright © 2008 Stephen Wade

British Library Cataloguing-in-Publication Data
A CIP record for this title is available from the British Library

ISBN 978 1 84114 697 3

HALSGROVE

Halsgrove House
Ryelands Business Park, Bagley Road,
Wellington, Somerset TA21 9PZ
Tel: 01823 653777
Fax: 01823 216796
email: sales@halsgrove.com
website: www.halsgrove.com

Printed and bound in India by
Parksons Graphics

This book is dedicated to Andy Wade

CONTENTS

ACKNOWLEDGEMENTS

For research purposes, thanks go to the members of the Stainforth, Thorne and Hatfield STH Forum. Also to particular people who have let me interview them or investigate their scenes of paranormal experience: Ady Cowell, Sarah, Claire, Jill and Irene in the library, and Tom Proctor. Tom Proctor and friends used to dig out aircraft from the Lindholme/Hatfield area, notably the finding of a floor from a Wellington bomber. His personal archive was very useful, and his account of 'Billy Lindholme' set me on the trail of that particular entity.

In compiling these ghostly narratives, I have been helped by many people, including Kate Walker, Paul Bellinger, Eileen and John Nichols, Virginia Mason, Joyce Young, Andy Owens and Rowland Cooper. Thanks also to those who responded to the call for recent experiences, notably Robert Collins, Jan Smith, Pat Holroyd, Enid Winkley, Maureen Ford, Philip Bolton and Jason Gibson. Most of the truly gripping stories here are previously unrecorded, and they often present the most rewarding reading experience.

PREFACE

BY IAN LAWMAN

Psychic medium and television celebrity

Paranormal investigations are booming now, like never before. Shows like *Most Haunted* and *I'm Famous and Frightened* have been such a huge success on TV; it's opened a massive market for paranormal groups to move forward with investigations.

Maybe it's become more difficult to be taken seriously, maybe because the paranormal is now more in the public eye, and that's opened the door to cranks and sceptics, so that makes it more difficult for genuine people who have an interest to take it seriously.

Regarding investigations, one of my personal favourites was at the Golden Fleece in York. It's a very active public house with dark and good souls.

Stephen Wade's *Hauntings in Yorkshire* will add more personal experiences for the records of paranormal events in the county.

INTRODUCTION

I was born in Leeds in 1948, and I have always been surrounded by stories. Most of the first ones were oral tales, told to me by my grandparents in a pre-television age. Of all these thrillers, one stands out, and I tell it in full in the first section. I was told that there was a ghost in the cellar in my grandparent's house. From that moment on, I was hooked on the paranormal.

Later, when I was a student at university, I had my first experience of the unexplained. In a room which was only dimly lit, I lay on a bed and felt a pressure by my leg, as if someone was sitting on the edge. I could see clearly the area by the window and the figure of an old man materialised, seemingly bending to touch something. I'm sure it was a man and a ghostly dog.

This book has stories of ghostly dogs, but these are much more fearful: the guytrash, or sometimes they are called bargests, appear to be around even now, and may be as much a part of the darker side of life as they were to the writer Charlotte Brontë, when she brings a tale of a spectral hound into her novel, *Jane Eyre*.

But the stories here are not from literature: they are from the street, told to me by people in conversation, or over the phone. This is a collection of uncanny, unexplained visitations from another world. This world sometimes laps over into that world we call everyday reality. When it does, we feel fear, but the record shows that only very rarely do spirits cause any physical harm. Of course, there are the entities we call poltergeists, and Colin Wilson has given probably the most exhaustive and gripping account of such a haunting in the case of the house in Pontefract in which a ghostly monk was seemingly making his presence felt.

My collected stories are from people just doing their jobs, or walking upstairs when they catch something out of the corner of their eye. Occasionally, experiences told have tallied with some documented accounts, such as the woman who saw the Blue Lady at Temple Newsam in the long gallery, thus confirming a well-established visitation.

I have my own workplace story, and this is in some ways a template for many that I collected. I was an office boy in a footwear company in 1963 in Leeds. I had been sent to deliver internal mail across to the warehouse. Walking over and up some stairs, I suddenly smelled a strong female perfume; turning round, I caught a glimpse of a woman looking incredibly like Cilla Black. But by the time I turned and was about to say hello, there was a whisper, and she was gone.

I told the tale to the office manager and he smiled. "Ah, you saw Ginger. Pretty isn't she? Been dead five years. I knew her well....Killed herself on that landing..."

People often ask me what constitutes evidence in these tales. The best way to illustrate my answer is to refer to my participation in a television programme in which a team of paranormal investigators went into well-known locations – it was *Derek Acorah's Ghosts Towns*. The weather was severely disruptive and one location that was planned had to be cancelled and Derek with his team had to go to an unexpected location. He was just as impressive there as anywhere else. In other words, information and stories in the public domain can, of course, be known before an investigation, but if sceptics think that mediums research a place before a visit, well, Derek's ability that night proves otherwise.

I am naturally always compiling paranormal stories and I am always keen to hear from people with genuine unexplained experiences – no matter where or when. Many of these tales come from phone calls after appeals for actual experience. I sifted and selected of course, but there can never be too many simply as raw material to work with and to research.

My thanks go to Christine Sitch at the Museums and Galleries Department, Leeds City Museums, for the use of the image of Temple Newsam.

The best paranormal stories are those we collect from actual everyday experience, and in gathering these tales, what has emerged is a sense that there are certain places that retain energy, places where there are resident entities who seem somehow to call to the living in some way we do not fully understand. The classic example of this in my own investigations has to be the hour I spent in an old factory in Leeds. I knew that it had been a place where there were once piece-workers back in the 1940s, young women who were using sewing machines for long hours every day. I sat alone and it was in semi-darkness. There was only a breeze outside in the late October evening. Then there was a steady invasion of sound, just a series of bursts like gun fire but somehow subdued, as if from another area hundreds of yards away. But then the sounds seemed to come into the walls and upstairs there were sounds of laughter and a radio, tinny and cheap, but distinctly a radio broadcast.

I did not stay there long. But I absolutely know that many people reading this will have had such experiences so I want to collect another volume to follow this. Yorkshire is indeed a large place – the 'broad acres' of old accounts by visitors. If there are fleeting but inexplicable experiences, I want to know about them. More than likely, they will not happen in old piles, castles and mansions: they will be poltergeists in modern semi-detached homes or figures walking along lanes, passages and alleys. The evidence is there for us, we just need to look harder.

A typical experience – one I have not written about separately in this book – was told to me by Maureen Ford, a student. She was working as a waitress in the Talbot pub in Malton when she saw the figure of a nun – as real as if she were alive today. She thought nothing of it until she mentioned it later. No-one else had seen the figure that day, though the room had been full of Sunday-lunchers at the time. Apparently she is seen by many, and there is a part of the pub known as the cloisters. That's the kind of happening most of us can identify with.

If you have any unworldly stories for me, please send them to this address, for inclusion in volume two:

Stephen.wade@ntlworld.com

GHOSTS AT HOME

Anyone who has ever experienced something uncanny going on in their own four walls will know that houses, like people, have their moods. The books and television programmes devoted to hauntings in the home repeatedly find similar phenomena: spirits who are present in a residual way, as an energy derived from a once-living person in the place, or as a visiting ghost: a spirit with a connection in life to the place.

There are many theories about how and why restless spirits haunt particular places. What is certain is that in cases where several people over a period of time have seen a similar shape, heard similar noises or experienced touch on the body from a presence, the pattern is convincing: more so than in isolated instances.

There are numerous well-documented cases of the latter in celebrated country homes or mansions, of course, and in the West Riding, one of the places with regular sightings is Temple Newsam, near Leeds. But what about the variety of unexplained visitations in the terraces, the semi-detached homes and in the flats, across the county?

Almost everyone I speak to in the course of paranormal research has a tale to tell: something inexplicable. In most cases, the behaviour of the ghost or poltergeist is at least partly explicable with reference to known events in the social history of the place in question.

In homes, the most common types of paranormal experience tend to be in the category of 'recently deceased' or 'limbo' sightings. In the former, a person grieving sees or hears something or someone strongly suggestive of the nature of the recently dead. In the latter, it is a case of historical research revealing an explanation of a possible haunting. I had many scraps of narrative, not sustained enough to use in this book, about people's sightings 'from the corner of the eye', of a relative recently dead, and many more recounting people being touched on the arm or being whispered to in places associated with a loved one just passed on.

But of course, there is also the rather more dramatic nature of homes as haunted places, and here social history plays its part. The Yorkshire textile towns, since their rapid development in the early years of the nineteenth century, have had a particular topography which plays a part in the following stories. Characteristic features of dozens of small towns and villages from Sowerby Bridge to Wetherby are those created by divisions of class and wealth coming along with the Industrial Revolution. Hence, a typical township will have rows of terrace houses, areas of semi-detached dwellings, and of course villas and town houses owned by the new progressive middle classes of the Victorian period.

A simple way to grasp this range of dwellings thrown together by historical processes is to drive from the M62 into Huddersfield along the Halifax Road. From the motorway into the town centre, one passes tiny stone terraces on the slopes; newer semis; flats (brand new) on Holly Bank, Lindley; grander, more spacious terraces, and also magnificent detached properties on the roadside between Lindley and the Technical College.

These factors mean that sightings of paranormal events have often occurred in dark courts and ginnels; but they have also happened in daylight, perhaps in a garden of a large Victorian villa. A man from Halifax told me that one summer day he looked up from his magazine out into the garden, where he saw a man working with a spade. He saw the figure take something from the ground and throw it towards the corner of the vegetable patch. When he ran out to see more clearly, the figure had gone. He asked about this among the neighbours, who had lived there many years. All facts pointed to the man being the gardener of the wealthy factory-owner who had once owned the house.

Of course, social and historical features also create a particular Yorkshire nature to most experiences. For instance, the former habit of keeping pigs at the end of the garden appears to be a common source of uncanny sightings. Several people told me that they still smell the presence of animals in straw, at the corner of the garden they have developed into a neat arbour or patio space.

Bramley Old Grouch

Lisa and Shelby had not been in their Bramley semi for very long. The first months had been a pleasure; setting up home, decorating, gardening, putting the imprint of their identity on the place. They had waited a long time for this sense of independence.

Then the music started. Neighbours close by were the type to enjoy inflicting their musical taste on anyone within hearing distance. This kind of experience is always potentially a cause of stress and disquiet. One morning, Lisa said that she didn't like the place any more, now that they had to live with such an annoyance.

From that moment on, the old grouch invaded the house. They would find towels that had been folded strewn across the bedroom floor; doors rattled when they were trying to relax; at times one of them would sense a figure standing by the doorway, only to vanish when words were spoken.

One day, as they were stepping into a taxi to take them into Leeds, Shelby noticed something moving in the window of the upstairs room. As they both looked, they saw an old man waving goodbye to them from the bedroom. Lisa told the taxi to wait and ran back inside. But at the door she stopped, suddenly overcome with panic.

It was the sign that they should go – permanently. The old grouch just didn't want them there.

The Man on the Stairs, Oakwood

Mrs Young had married a travelling salesman some years before they moved into the Oakwood area of Leeds. Formerly, she had owned a clothes shop, and now she was moving into a comfortable new semi in the suburbs, not far from Roundhay Park.

Life was not kind to her: her husband suffered a stroke and after a short illness, died.

Harry was a man who asserted himself in the house; one might say that he was the type to obsess about the condition of his living space. Somehow, he always seemed to be fussing about where and how to sit, where and how to eat, the state of the garden, the colour-scheme.

So maybe, with hindsight, it came as no surprise that, only weeks after his death, Mrs Young was opening the front door to go into the garden when she sensed something behind her. She turned, looked up the stairs, and saw what she describes as Harry but with his outline fuzzy like a picture out of focus and, for a split second, she saw his face in the centre of the shape, smaller than in life, but distinguishable.

She was understandably shocked, but the vision lasted such a short time that she was soon reflecting on this and working to recover some sense of reality. It happened a second time just a short while later. She recalls whispering to herself that she wanted him to go and leave her to take care of the house.

It seems to have worked, as he never came a third time.

Hanging Man in Luddenden

Cathy Curry was given a memory of one of the most disturbing hauntings one could ever imagine. This was thirty years ago, in a house in Luddenden Foot, close to St Walburga's church. The name of 'Walburga' relates to 'Walpurgisnacht' – the night before May Day when the witches were supposed to be rampant, working their spells. Although Walburga was an English nun, and so the link with a church in a quiet part of England was understandable and nothing to do with witches, what Cathy was told about this day was so shocking that she has never forgotten it.

Her friend was fond of playing the piano in this house. She liked to play in a space below a large gilt-framed wall mirror. Usually, while playing, she would occasionally glance up above her to see the reflection of a vase of flowers. It made her feel good to see the blaze of colour as she was caught in the mood of the music.

But one day she glanced up and saw, not the flowers, but the grimace of a face in the throes of great pain: after a few seconds of staring at the is face, she saw that it was a woman hanging in a noose.

The Playmate, Sowerby Bridge

Susan used to feel drawn to a small store-cupboard under the stairs in the large Edwardian detached house she lived in when she was a child. It was a house with dozens of rooms, most of them full of light from huge windows. But she was attracted, she recalls, to this dark closet because her friend Thomas used to call for her. Only, as she now knows for sure, Thomas was not a real, living person.

'Even now, I sometimes think it was just a mad thing... a kid's imagi-nation... but then I piece it all together and I just know it was something that actually happened to me...' she says today.

Thomas was tall, thin, maybe of around ten years of age. He had curly fair hair and wore a brown suit with short trousers, Susan brings to mind. Usually, when he visited, it was when she was alone in a room and the adults were busy in other rooms. Both her parents were professional people, and always busy on some project, or away from home visiting. At such times there would be a faint calling of her name from downstairs, and then, if she tried to ignore it, soon there would be a whispering in the doorway. 'Susan… come and play with me…. Do come!'

Susan says the words with a shiver, but then with a laugh of release. Whenever she talks of Thomas she still feels that people are going to laugh it off, just put it down to childhood, when we talk to ourselves.

'But you know…. He touched my sleeve… and he told some old stories, they were Shakespeare stories some of them, but in old-fashioned language.'

Of course, she told her parents that she had been playing with Thomas. Their usual response was to tell her to visit friends more often. It was all put down to her being a lonely, only child. He has not called to her since they left when she was fifteen. I asked, does she think he is still in that house? But it has been demolished, apparently.

Where did little Thomas go then?

Quarry Hill Flats Sprite

If you visit the West Yorkshire Playhouse today, and you park on one of the areas behind, you will most likely have no idea that the expanse of land around you, stretching across to the roundabout by Millgarth police station and behind as far as the bottom end of Potternewton, was once occupied by a vast housing complex called Quarry Hill Flats. These were built in the years 1935 –1941, designed by Charles Jenkinson, and were planned on the template of the Karl Marx Hof building in Vienna.

All this was very 'modern' at the time, and seemed to be part of a futuristic vision for the working class and their lifestyles in the city. But things went wrong; the place deteriorated. By the 1960s, parts of the area were inhabited by suspicious characters and it was proving to be a tough place to live, as well as a hard place to police.

It seems that, as well as delivery people and official visitors, other beings of a less welcome nature visited some of the rooms at Quarry Hill. One particular corner, which would have stood directly facing the bus station, had a presence that can only be called a sprite. This is because it was mischievous. From one perspective, it has to have been a poltergeist. It threw objects across rooms, and that was in several different adjacent flats; people were thrown against the wall; radio sets were a special target for attack, several being destroyed.

This might not be so unusual, except that it appears that the sprite did not disappear along with the brick and concrete. Passers-by walking across the car-park area have reported hearing whispers; objects sometimes move along by themselves when there is no breeze.

One Loiner, a delivery man and van driver, says there was always something suspect about the whole bus station area and the flats opposite; he puts it down to the attacks and murders that took place by the Parish Church. One of my own uncles told me a tale of seeing a figure in a black suit walk across to the flats from the bus station, as my uncle was waiting for a bus, but the figure faded away into dust before reaching the other side.

'There's bad blood around that neck of Leeds, I'll tell you. Don't walk that land alone late at night... I believe ghouls walk abroad there....'

Heptonstall: William Clarke

In the Dog and Partridge Inn, Heptonstall, in 1899, there was a very suspicious death, unsolved to this day. William Clarke, a stonemason, settled into the inn for an afternoon and evening of drinking and enjoy-ing the company of women. The long session was to end in his death, and he was more than likely a murder victim.

Clarke was found dying in the street, and had clearly fallen (or been pushed) from a high window. The official line was that he had tried to climb out of an attic window while intoxicated, but several circumstances point to the fact that this would have been impossible without someone seeing him and, more, he had been robbed.

All in all, it was a violent death, and it might come as no surprise to learn that in 1963, when Peter Harvey was living in the property (no longer a pub but a private dwelling) he had an uncanny experience.

Peter says that he slept in the attic and this was obviously a dangerous place, with plenty of nooks and crannies. On a windy night, Peter made his way downstairs and fell heavily, breaking his leg. He says that the attic was always a place with an unsettling atmosphere, full of creaks and groans, and maybe these sounds were not always the wind. When Peter learned of a more famous fall in that building, it certainly filled him with misgivings. We might even say there was a hex on the room.

Beeston Streets Spirit

The vast stretch of Beeston in South Leeds covers Dewsbury Road as far as the slopes down to Mill Shaw, and to the west just before the walk to Elland Road football ground there used to be many old red-brick streets, built in the early years of the twentieth century. They were reminders of the world of poverty in the 1930s, when many poor families had to live from hand to mouth and with regular visits to the pawn shop.

Talking to older or former residents of these streets, it became apparent that there was something malevolent abroad in the wars years and after, particularly around South Ridge Street. One memory is of a cellar beneath the end house on this street of large Victorian semi-detached houses. They all had attics and cellars. In these dark basements there would be a coal-cellar and a food store. I was told that a man who was an ARP Warden in the war reported investigating this cellar and, walking into the pitch darkness, became aware of something or someone watching him. His instinct was to brave it out and bellow into the place where he heard a shuffling noise

The only response he had was a murmuring sounding like *Not yours to say...Not yours...* He was a big man, normally difficult to unnerve. But he was out of there very sharp. In the same street, other people spoke of a whispering in their ears while walking at night. It is easy to imagine how especially terrifying this was in the war black-out. One lady recalls her sister coming home bruised from walking into a lamp-post in the black out, but her main distress was caused not by the physical pain but by what she called 'The thin woman with the lisp.'

Beeston, in its old form, has been the subject of Tony Harrison's film-poem, *V.* He made a point of telling us about the defaced graves in the cemetery. For sure unpleasant things have happened in those streets, but nothing so unsettling as the little frail spirit who likes to whisper in the dark.

16

One Legged Ghost on Selby Road

Andy is clear about his meeting with the woman. It was late one night, as he was leaving the Wykebeck Arms on the Selby Road. He was about to walk home towards Halton Moor and it was late, quiet for a Thursday night. It was autumn and there was a strong wind. Leaves were being blown into his face. Then he knows he heard a voice calling him and turned towards the corner of the car park. He swears he saw the outline of a woman of middle age. She was short and wiry, all in white. But the odd thing was, she had only one leg.

As usual in such cases, the approach is to look into the local history. Sure enough, many years ago, it seems it was around 1960, a milk delivery woman was hit by a tram near the pub. People say she lost a leg. As to the white appearance, could it have been her smock? Andy likes to think so, though it was a shape that appeared insubstantial to him, as if someone was stepping out of a dense mist. The most frustrating thing for him is that he cannot recall what she said.

Was this a restless spirit haunting the place of a violent death? The only sure thing is that Andy had only drunk one pint of beer that night. He was keen to get home to watch the soaps, so his mind was clear.

The Gaiety Regular

At the lower end of Chapeltown in Leeds, towards Harehills, one of the true landmarks used to be the 'Gaiety Kinema' as it announced itself to passers-by: ornate, decadent and eye-catching. The building had its classy period. But it had less pleasant connections in more recent times, as it was frequented by the Yorkshire Ripper, and indeed, as it is on the fringes of the red light district, the area is not always an entirely comfortable place to be.

But not all of its visitors were alive and of this time, it seems. Reports tell of a brooding man seen in a corner, most markedly at late morning; it has been hard to find any story behind this, but he also seemed to dislike people pulling pints, as if he were some kind of moral presence. Mrs Calverley, who lived on one of the streets opposite, the Bayswaters, may have some kind of answer as to who he was. She says that he was a lodger once; she reports seeing him about three months after his death, a man with a very lined face, quite stern, and wearing a waistcoat and fob-watch as in the thirties and forties.

The story goes that he was called Harold and liked to dance. Some witnesses say that Harold would dance late at night by the packed bar, and that he was also seen sometimes at a pub up beyond Harehills, at Gipton. Here we have a happy ghost: there are no accounts of him harming or scaring anyone.

Crossgates Shadow

Turning from Selby Road up towards Crossgates and by Killingbeck Hospital, drivers in Leeds would be oblivious of the supposed evil presence under the viaduct leading from the lower part of Wykebeck Valley Road across to the streets between the coal-tips and Selby Road. Under here, in the shadows of the brickwork, people have felt some kind of unwelcome presence. The ghost was prevalent in the 1960s and 1970s in particular, when people who were children then have given accounts of playing near the arches and having a feeling that they were being watched. There seems to be no explanation, but some residents living there in those years say it is the unhappy spirit of a worker killed when the place was built many years before.

A man who went to Osmondthorpe School in the sixties recalls sensing a shape moving about in the shade as he played marbles with his friend. 'I know I ran home to my mam sharpish and told her I was being followed.' He smiles now, but there was nothing amusing about the viaduct ghoul.

Harehills Haunting

The Leeds that is disappearing in the face of modernity was a place of almost endless rows of redbrick terraces, and each suburb had its particular features and identity. But as the streets came down under the demolition balls, and the past was battered down to oblivion, restless, unhappy souls had to find somewhere to go. We have to wonder where the little girl living in one of the streets between Easterly Road and Harehills went.

She would have to go somewhere, as she was a spirit tied to a few square feet of living space, and her presence was intense. Mr Matlin, who lived there many years ago, says he could write a book on Little Sally as he calls her. 'That golden haired lass used to giggle or chuckle… you'd be listening to the wireless, all quiet else, and then you'd hear this laugh like a kid playing… in the corner.'

His wife and two sons both spoke about seeing the little girl indistinctly but definitely there, and one son feels sure that the ghost was maimed in some way. He swears that her face was disfigured.

In that small house, in those walls, Sally was in a sort of limbo, perhaps, a resident presence, but now maybe in the open spaces. It is a story that reminds us yet again how much a home for the living is also inhabited by those who have passed across to the next world, yet leave a residual occupancy, hating the thought of letting go of the place that was their paradise, maybe.

Exorcism in Cleckheaton

Pat Holroyd had an encounter with a ghost over thirty years ago, and she will never, ever forget it. She was living in a downstairs flat in Scholes, and had been there for three months when she notes that 'silly things happened'. In the home were herself and her six-month old son, and it was impossible to get warm, even with a high fire. She would go to the shops, and on coming back, she would find a bed made earlier that morning now un-made.

Things became worse: drawers would be opened, objects would move about the room. She thought it must be her imagination, but then she was sure that no-one was breaking in. Then there came the actual appearance of the spirit. She woke one morning at two o'clock and looked across to her son's cot. Above the cot was a figure in a mist, 'like a haze… nothing you could touch,' Pat says.

The figure walked across to the bed where she was lying, lifted a cover and got in. She was struggling to shout but could not speak. She says she tried to yell for someone to come, but she could make no sound at all. 'I was frozen with fear,' Pat says. It seems that she passed out after this horrendous sight.

The next day she gathered all their belongings and left the flat. Her mother thought she had imagined it all, but eventually agreed to go back with her. They built up a fire, and a little girl of the family was playing in the middle of the room, as a gust of wind arrived from nowhere. The girl froze with fear; the dog darted for cover under a sideboard. Pat's cousin, Richard, was sitting in a chair and tried to stand up to help, but says he felt paralysed by some unknown force pressing on him.

When eventually he rose and forced a window open, everyone realised that the pram, which had been standing in the room, had been pushed all the way to the end of a corridor. That was the last straw. It was time to see a priest.

Pat and family went to see the local priest and he asked the obvious questions about whether they had been using a ouija board or otherwise dabbling in things unknown. Finally, he came to the house to see for himself. There was no doubt in his mind: he was left alone in the flat for forty minutes, and when Pat returned, he talked about there being an unsettled spirit there, someone who had died in unhappy circumstances.

The priest did a service and blessed each room in turn. He said that the spirit had been gaining strength and had reached the stage where it could shift quite large and solid things. Everyone involved attended a ceremony for a blessing in the church and, soon after, there was peace in the home.

Pat today talks about what she actually saw: 'It was the form of a person... not a male or female, not an identifiable being... just a form.' She had previously always been sceptical and scoffed at such accounts of the paranormal. But now it was different. She had seen and felt a presence beyond full explanation.

The Photo-Frame

Enid Winkley has a tale to tell of a photo-frame that did something that defies explanation. It was in Hull, in 1943, and the story begins with a garden party; Enid and some friends recall a sunny day and a stroll around the stalls, and what caught her eye most was a picture frame, costing five shillings. She remembers the frame as being quite beautiful, and as she was earning just £2 a week, five shillings was a lot to pay, so when she bought the frame, she was sure it was something she really wanted.

Enid told me, 'A postcard sized photograph would fit in it nicely... the frame lined with deep blue velvet... The front of the frame was embossed, filigree silver. It was the loveliest frame I had ever seen.' Later that day, she picked a photo of her best friend, Anna, sitting on a chair wearing a blue top and pleated plaid skirt. Enid says, 'Her hair was full of ringlets, not reaching her shoulders. Anna had a lovely big smile for the camera. I was pleased with the colouring I had worked on the snapshot.'

But only a day after the picture was put in the frame, Enid brings to mind the shock that was waiting for her. 'I thought my eyes were playing tricks on me' she told me. There, in place of Anna's picture was another picture – a child of a bygone age. The photo was sepia and the girl seemed to be around fourteen; she sat on a high-backed chair, ornate with carving and slender frame. Her softly waved and ringleted hair was waist-long, topped with a huge satin bow on her head. Her expression, says Enid. Was 'of haunting sadness, and I felt sad looking at it.'

She kept looking at the photo, then turning away, expecting the old image to have vanished, but it did not disappear. Enid thought she was going crazy. It took her four days to share the experience. She decided to test things and asked Anna who was in the photo. Pointing to the picture, Anna said, 'A school girl.'

'What is she wearing?'

'A pretty dress, and she has long hair and a big bow in it.'

Enid recalls that Anna didn't seem to realise that she should have been in the frame.

The end of the tale is that Enid could take no more: she went out to the dustbin and threw the frame in it. She reflects that, 'Looking back I think I should have taken it to the vicar to see if he could tell me more, or do something about it… I always felt that this child in the picture needed help, and she was still waiting for help. I just couldn't live with that frame.'

The Cottingham Cyclist

Cottingham, a village between Hull and Beverley, is still a very attractive place – one of those locations we see when the traffic has gone and the older buildings and parkland are enjoyed for what they are. As you drive towards the University of Hull from the M62 Leeds direction, you may well drive through Cottingham and see the old pubs like The Railway, and some of the older and attractive homes, some now converted to halls of residence for students.

There have been some dark deeds around the place – even the most idyllic spots usually have their murder stories. There was a terrible attack on a woman in her own home there, back in Hallgate, in 1901. But the poor woman there who took a year to die is not the most prominent restless spirit in Cottingham. That dubious honour goes to a lady in black who is seen on her bicycle. The sightings seem to have started in the 1980s when a local cyclist took a short cut through a passage that joins Link Road and Newgate Street.

What happened was that the cyclist saw another cyclist – but from an age long gone. The cyclist was a woman, wearing black, and riding an old sit up and beg style of bike. But on a second glance, the figure had gone.

Investigations and enquiries have led to some other encounters with this spectre; a student reported, just two years ago, that she had been looking in a shop window when she caught the sight of a 'floating dark figure' behind in the reflection, something seeming to be floating on air. But when she turned she saw the black-dressed cyclist, just for a few seconds, before the shape seemed to blur.

Another sighting was by the level crossing where the train from Hull out to the coast dashes through Cottingham. It was dusk and the traffic had eased when a cyclist recalled sensing that another bike was coming behind him. He heard the gentle thrumming noise and turned to look, but when he saw a woman in black who 'looked like she was on the set of a costume drama' his heart missed a beat and then he said hello. But on that word, the figure dissolved.

The Wet Feet

It happened on one day in the long dry summer. There was no reason or explanation that seemed viable. But it was something that to this day the family cannot explain and their eyes are wide and mouths open when they recall the uncanny sight they saw thirty years ago when they came home from a holiday.

They lived in an ordinary semi-detached in Huddersfield. Dad worked for the railway and mum looked after the three children. Their house was fairly new, so what they saw was not something that could have been looked up in the local archives to see if some awful tale of death was the root cause of what they had seen.

Mum, dad and the children trudged home a few hundred yards after a long journey home from Filey, by train and then bus. They walked up the drive and opened the door. Mum said, 'Tea I think.'

She busied herself in the kitchen while the kids sat on the sofa and dad unpacked a case, looking for something. Then the daughter screamed and said, 'Look there dad!'

She pointed to the lino by the table and as heads turned, they saw wet footprints being made, as if a child was walking from the table to them. They instinctively moved to one side, and then mum came in, hearing the shrieks. She saw the marks as well.

'The weird thing was, the next day, we were outside, gardening, when there they were again. It was dry – no rain at all. So I saw the footprints and shouted for everybody to look' said dad.

It took weeks of nervous watching and waiting, staring at the same places where they had seen the prints. But they never came again.

'I just remember being scared' the daughter recalls, 'But after that few days, there was nothing again. The house is still there, but I wouldn't want anyone to know.'

SPIRITS & POLTERGEISTS
AT WORK & PLAY

Visitations from the other world to places of work have a particular interest; unlike ghosts in private dwellings, many of these beings seem attached to something linked to a daily routine or a passion for a trade or craft. That odd but strong pull towards a place of work we see in life appears to exist in spirits too, and of course, if the souls are residual presences connected with a painful death or a tragic accident, that only serves to add to the interest. Charles Dickens fastened on to this feature of life when he wrote his best-known ghost story, *The Signalman*, and some of these tales are of railway hauntings. But such uncanny experiences can happen anywhere, any time.

Hebden Bridge Spectre

Philip Bolton was working as a signalman at Hebden Bridge in the sixties, and on his Sunday night shift he saw something that he has never forgotten. The nature of the work then meant that the gap of time from eleven at night until five the next morning needed filling, and of course, it wouldn't do to fall asleep. So the time had to be spent somehow. Philip comments that he even learned to play the banjo in these times.

But the twilight hours are often when people see things that they are not too sure about. On one particular night he was listening to the radio and smoking his pipe. A mere glance along the platform through his window was enough to catch sight of a figure in white. He says it was 'brilliant', first hanging around outside his box, and then reappearing at the top of the stairs – and bear in mind that this meant it came through the closed door. It then stood close to him, right at his side.

As Philip comments, 'To say that I needed the toilet quick is an understatement.' He sat and tried to come to terms with what he thought he had just seen. He had instinctively turned the light on when it came close; what he can't say for certain is whether or not he simply dreamt he had the experience.

But the latter idea seems very unlikely when we note that Philip talks of another signalman he met two years later, a man in his late twenties, with a young family, who was working the same shift. In this case, though, the reaction was very different; he had seen the same apparition, but rung the police about it, and also told all his workmates. A policeman had come to help, and eventually joked, 'Well, what shall I do – arrest it?'

The young man might have tried to laugh it off with all the others now discussing the event, but at six the next morning, he left his box and resigned. Philip rightly questions whether he and the other man saw the same thing. It seems highly likely. Maybe what the other man saw was something even more unnerving – after all, what would need to happen to make a man resign on the spot and never want to go back to that workplace?

Jonah Marr – Huddersfield

Being a railway porter at the magnificent Victorian station on George Square, Huddersfield, is reputed to be a perilous occupation at times, and the reason why lies in the bizarre injury and disappearance of Jonah Marr, a porter there who had an accident and whose spirit lives on in a malevolent and impish way.

Jonah was skilled at prising or cajoling tips out of wealthy travellers, and records show that he was not popular with his peers. There must have been something unpleasant about him because when he was knocked accidentally down ono the line and lay with both legs broken, no-one moved with any alacrity to help him in his predicament. Jonah was not really mended fully after such a serious fall, and was a pathetic, rather mal-formed figure afterwards.

Tradition has it that the time of his fall, 11.25 a.m., is the time that the station clock used to stop every day for some while after the tragedy. But more disturbing is the frequency of reports about small accidents happening to workers there. Stories tell of people being nudged, pinched or distracted so that minor accidents tended to happen.

People have also reported feeling cold sensations on their skin, and even the menacing sound of laughter, vague but there, somewhere. The possibility of any resolution to all this is as distant as the hope of ever finding out what Jonah's destiny was: we have no idea where he ended his days. But it looks like his spirit resides there, where he spent most of his days on earth.

The St James's Nurse

Two security guards at Jimmy's – St James's Hospital in Leeds – have confirmed what common sense would tell any paranormal investigator: that places where sick people often spend a long time dying are places where ghosts tend to loiter. The hospital covers a broad area, its boundaries extending into the Harehills area at one side, and down towards Potternewton at the other. The campus had many dark corners, and some forgotten places. Such a place is the old link-passage to a ward that was up and running in the sorrowful days of the Great War.

The guards were checking out some suspicious sounds one night, as they were on their rounds, and from this place that was a store-room at the time, they heard sounds of movement and low voices. Suspecting a break-in, they opened up and shone a torch in: to their astonishment, they saw the figure of a nurse dressed in grey and white. She seemed as real as anyone else they had seen that day, but then she faded away.

Andy and John are not keen on venturing into that room again. If there are some residual energies there of past medics, then let them carry on caring. Their presence might unintentionally harm the living, otherwise.

The Woman in Black, Southowram

This lofty part of Calderdale not only has the ghost of the Manor House pub at Bank Top, haunted by a spirit called locally Blithe Sarah, a grandmother of a former licensee in 1922, but more prominently, as writer Andy Owens recalls, the woman in black in the aisle of the Wesleyan Methodist Church.

Derek Rhodes was eager to film his niece's wedding in 1983 and was pleased to be able to use his video camera. But looking at the video on playback, there was the figure of a woman in black standing among the guests.

There have been other ghostly images caught on video, notably a woman walking in a corridor caught on a video film taken at St

Margaret's, Beverley, eight years ago. But very few of these are preserved or properly examined. The Southowram case is surely one with enough witnesses to make it of special interest to ghost-hunters.

Obviously, the logical questions were asked: did anyone know her? Was she a guest? But the local journalists were wanting to know more, and Mr Rhodes could only say that the figure was more clearly a funeral guest – dressed entirely in black, including a veil over her face. On the image, she is apparently speaking, which adds yet more mystery. Nothing was discovered in terms of sources or origins in historical reference after the uncanny image was captured. Andy Owens notes the frustrating fact that the family moved away after this, their video going with them. So, as Andy has already asked, does anyone know where Mr Rhodes is today? Does he still have this film?

Police Stations

Restless spirits might be expected to haunt police stations, and although source material is scarce, there are some intriguing tales here. In Millgarth, Leeds, there were always tall tales recounted which are urban myths, such as the notion that there was a tunnel leading from the pub at the bottom of the Headrow to the cells. But there have been tales of voices heard crying and shouting there, where no-one is present.

More definite are the tales of the Calderdale stations. In the nineteenth century, there was a long discussion throughout Calderdale about the development of a rural police force, and this was twenty years after Robert Peel's first 'bobbies' appeared. From 1863 the police headquarters here were in the basement of the new Town Hall. Although the Hall has its own stories, there seem to be uncanny tales of some substance based on the Prescott Street station. This opened in the seventies, and there are reports of officers hearing whistling, doors opening and closing of their own volition, and even the standard phenomenon of hauntings, the cold spot.

Most substantiated of these is the occurrence of a ringing noise in the cells, and the sound of feet shuffling in cell corners when they are vacant. One thing these tales do confirm is the theory that past sounds are held in the physical limits of an enclosed space.

A long catalogue of investigations in prisons, workhouses, houses of correction and county gaols seems to assert this feature.

Cooper Bridge, Mirfield

The Three Nuns inn at Mirfield takes its name from three holy sisters, Alice Raggio, Elizabeth Hopton and Joan Meton. As with the mystery surrounding the death of Robin Hood at nearby Kirklees Priory, there is an old legend about them, concerning their business of a hostelry in the years after the priory was ransacked in the mid sixteenth century.

The pub has a long history of uncanny events, and there may be a root of these in the person of the notorious Elizabeth de Stainton, the nun who is supposed to have brought about Robin's death, as an old narrative poem relates. It is hard to avoid these religious personages as there is the sign painted in the Victorian period, showing the three nuns, and there is even a painting of Elizabeth herself.

But what has actually gone on there? Some reckon that there was a hex on the place, and that this was linked with the discovery of a strange ram's head behind a fireplace when building was in progress. The head was not put back in its place, and many would hold the view that this was a causative event with some foreboding attached. Years ago there were countless inexplicable happenings in the place, such as beer taps turned on without human action; objects such as plates would move, and doors would inexplicably open and close.

Sure enough, after a former landlord reported all this to his brewery, the head of the ram was put back where it was found, and things settled down again. But Rowland Cooper paid a visit to the new landlord recently, and was told that a guest had insisted he was being watched by a tall grey figure with a beard. Rowland also notes that a mirror had fallen from a wall and smashed.

Anecdotes from drinkers around Huddersfield suggest that this is not unusual for inns and hostelries in the area: the general line of thought is that this particular corner of the White Rose county has a fair number of spirits who might have moved on, but who still feel the convivial pull of the local and the regulars.

Two Pubs, Bingley

Of all the Yorkshire pubs and inns with reputedly eerie atmospheres or unknown visitors, the Bingley Arms must take the lead for sheer antiquity and the right milieu for visitations. William Faulkner once said that the past is always present and in fact was never past, and in this tranquil dell in Bardsey it is not difficult to see what the American writer meant.

This is because the Bingley Arms is in a quiet village centre, with other old properties around, and a churchyard. It nestles in greenery and somehow has a dignity and a presence, as if it welcomes you but offers more than meets the eye. I was there in early 2004 and asked people about the village, and was told that this idyllic spot once had a pillory. In fact, the site of the inn, way back in the early Medieval period, was used as a court, and the malefactors arraigned there did not have far to go before they were pilloried. There is no surprise that glimpses of past times crossing the present occur here, as the core of the place is very old indeed; some say that the heart of the building is pre-1000 AD.

Stories often relate to objects moving and mysterious sounds, but the central story is about a supposed rape of a young woman here many years ago; she killed herself on the premises and people have reported seeing a young girl dressed in a black dress sitting in a chair in the taproom.

The Old White Horse is also very ancient, and its main claim to fame is that John Wesley preached here, standing on some steps outside the inn. Again, the place was once used as an instrument of the law, and maybe this accounts for some evidence of restless souls here. Customers have recorded the experience of intensely cold areas, localised, as often happens with this phenomenon. There have also been whispers heard and sometimes, it appears, even a figure seen at times – reputedly the ghost of a man who died of a seizure near the fireplace.

Bradford Paper Hall

This is the oldest building in Bradford, and only just managed to survive after a serious deterioration thirty years ago. Mystery surrounds its origins and even its name. One viewpoint is that it was built in the Civil War period. But it has been preserved and has a noble aspect and a solidity about it. Just to observe the building is to sense a troubled presence there, and indeed it has had a notable haunting, according to Marie Campbell.

This was the apparition of an admiral who committed suicide in the place, and was first seen (or at least the first report was given) as long ago as 1884. The figure is supposed to be terrifying, with staring eyes.

Sounds have also been heard at night, and a mumbling voice apparently adding up a column of figures. There have now been several sightings of a figure outside, also, a shape in white or silver. 'An historical figure' is the phrase normally used.

If all these spirits are the sad admiral, then the story should be open to research and some kind of verification, but it has resisted investigation. These frustrations are not that uncommon in this context, either. Places of murder or suicide often reveal a continuing effort to 'hush up' the truth behind the death, and it may be the case in the Paper Hall ghost.

Calderdale Pubs

Journalist Virginia Mason and Ghost Walk leader Paul Bellinger both have lots of tales to tell about the many interesting pubs and inns of Calderdale. These are not always unnerving or nasty; some are humorous and entertaining in a surreal way at times. One of the most atmospheric is the Blue Ball Inn at Soyland, a place which no longer exists; it has been converted into flats. But in the eighteenth century a serving girl there was raped by Iron Will, a notorious character in the area. Not only did he rape her, but he then drowned her in a pool in a wild place. The story is that her voice can still be heard, fearful of the attack.

The Ring o' Bells in Halifax reputedly has a ghost called Wally, who was walking this earth in the seventeenth century; there is a gravestone in the cellar which some think is linked to Wally. But this is nothing compared with The Fleece in Elland.

The Fleece has its residual spiritual energy in the shape of Old Leathery Coit, a beggar murdered there. His story ascends to the level of a legend, as he is reckoned to drive a coach, and he is headless for this task.

In terms of humour and quaintness, it is hard to beat the tale of Hilda, a ghost at the Grove Inn, Brearley, Luddenden, who cooks bacon and eggs. Hilda used to be a cook for the nearby brewery workers. But one fateful day poor Hilda went down into the cellar, never to surface again. Val Watts notes that there was a well down there: was that her destiny – to die in that deep darkness, her cries unheard?

Such is the welcoming cordiality and cosiness of the Yorkshire pub that it is understandable that a spiritual presence would be reluctant to leave the geographical centre of most contentment in life. But Calderdale pubs appear to have a glut of paranormal tales attached. The former pub called The Pineapple, I was told by a local shop-owner with an interest in local history, was frequented by actors in the days when there was a theatre by the North Bridge. He recalls being told by his father that the ghost of a woman was often seen, and heard weeping outside The Pineapple. Plenty of violence and some murders took place there in Victorian times. Maybe she was a victim of one of these. Characters treading the boards in those days were a volatile lot, in a precarious occupation, then considered only one step away from a criminal lifestyle.

If there ought to be a haunting of a restless spirit, it should be in the Old Cock Inn. Here the Coiner David Hartley was apprehended. But more commonly reported hauntings associated with the Coiners tend to be from Heptonstall, and indeed a brutal murder took place there, when a turncoat was brutally killed by some of his former associates. Rarely have murder and haunting, obviously inextricably linked, been so dramatically present as in the old pre-Victorian inns of Calderdale; they each have their own identity and sense of community, indicative of a phase in our social history when togetherness had a profound impor-tance for the working people.

Boggard Farm

A boggard is what we more usually call a goblin or an evil sprite – see the Boggart Hill story in this section. The word is most likely from the Welsh 'bwg' – a ghost. In some parts of Britain the boggard is more closely defined as non-human rather than the ghost of a person once living in a specific place. There are those who consider a boggard to be an elemen-tal, a spirit from the atmosphere and from nature, not animal or human in origin.

In 1831 a farm at Bierley was called Boggard Farm, and that name is itself suggestive of something gone wrong in the history of the plot, some malevolence about the place. There are countless lanes and roads around the local townships of our land with names like 'Boggart Hill' and the reasons for the name are lost in antiquity, but there is no doubt that this farm was inhabited by some force of evil. In that year, Mrs Kay was buried in the Cleckheaton congregational chapel.

When the new owner took over, a Mr Frith, there commenced a long and disturbing series of sounds, movements and feelings of unease about the house. Sounds of the rustling noises we hear when dresses are folded emanated; bolts rattled on doors; there was even a woman's voice heard, and some said it was the spirit of Mrs Kay. The farm became a notorious place for folk to come and gawp at, intrigued at the stories being circulated. Even ghost-hunters and ministers who came to investigate were frightened away.

A certain Rev. Frith (not related to the owner) tried to perform an exorcism, and spoke to the spirit, assuming the presence was indeed Mrs Kay. But nothing came of this, despite a sound of a chair being tapped. History relates that several others came to try out their fortitude and survive a night at the farm, but few succeeded. One guest even tried to shoot what he thought was a ghost there. It appears that we have a case of one of the first media frenzies, here, in this quiet part of Yorkshire, as it would have been in the early decades of the nineteenth century.

But no full explanation has been put forward nor are we certain that the visitor was Mrs Kay. The name suggests that there had been uncanny activity there on the site long before Mrs Kay passed away. Most evidence points to the presence of a poltergeist, and hence more likely a boggard – one whose activities may be as ancient as the settlement itself.

Gasworks Spectre, Huddersfield

The crowds walking down towards the McAlpine Stadium on a Saturday, taking the familiar route past the gasworks and over the canal past Hartwell Ford, will mostly have little idea that the road and canal bank are the haunt of a ghost who is most likely a suicide from the Victorian period.

This is reportedly Old Joe, a canal worker who ended it all after suffering a desperately chronic illness which stopped him being able to earn his money. Joe, apparently drunk and out of his senses, plunged in by the canal bridge opposite the Gas Works Club where Huddersfield fans gather before the match today. He has been seen by workers walking along the wasteland beneath the gasworks, sometimes humming a tune. Many have reported hearing a man humming late at night, when the pubs are closing; others have seen a shadowy figure entering the water but never making a splash: it is simply a re-enactment of the old man's death.

When seen, Joe has had a limp and walks with great effort. His spine was bending and all his strength was gone when he ended his life. He always has a stick when sighted.

When I asked a man who knew of the ghost what he had to say about the tale, all he said was that a kingfisher lives by the waters, even in the rubbish thrown in there; fancifully, he wondered if the bird might be old Joe's spirit. The only sure thing is that the atmosphere around that canal is dour and grey; there is an eerie silence there, and as you stand and contemplate how different the world is from Joe's, you feel you hear that humming behind you and the tap of his stick.

Sweat Shop Ghost

Two women who used to work at a dressmaking factory in Leeds, a building on the left as you drive to the beginning of the M1 South from Leeds, have a worrying tale to tell about their years making dresses there. The place is no longer a factory, but looks strangely out of place in its setting, among the modern, high and busy new centre of Leeds as it has been radically changed by development to cope with motorway traffic.

Audrey Slack remembers one time when a shadow passed through the room as she was in the toilet there. Many others said they had seen a shape of a man in a corner, and heard a voice sobbing. Audrey was told that a man had died there once, after cutting an artery in an accident. The story was that he had been acting the goat with some scissors.

Liz has a memory of a 'shape' apparently standing looking at her, seen from the corner of her eye as she was working hard at some piece-work. 'I know I was over-tired at the time... my eyes were fuzzy, but I swear I wasn't imagining it. I felt his eyes piercing like needles, into me...'

It's hard to imagine such things in that dark, unremarkable building. But the ghost could still be around there now, restless and yet unable to leave that place of its death, even with the traffic so close and the modern world so loud and hurried.

Seacroft Spectre

The industrial estate by the side of the ring road in Leeds, heading towards Crossgates, has had clusters of buildings on both sides for over thirty years now, and many things have changed. The firms have changed names; some newer places have arrived. But one part of this area survives untouched since the late 1960s, when, according to a man who worked in a warehouse then, a very menacing spirit was wandering on a path.

The path is there today, leading from the ring road across to a parallel road and past a sports ground. When Roy was working there, he recalls an old red-brick place no bigger than a shed on the path, and that is where he saw the ghost walk in. 'It was like a filmy cloud... a mist, but with a sort of dark core, maybe a small dark face at the centre of this mist.'

He was walking back from eating a sandwich in his dinner break, and going back to what was then Saxone Shoes' warehouse and offices. Quite a few of the workers would wander across for a stroll there and spend some time away from desks or shelves. But Roy can remember that shiver that went through him when he just felt something behind him, slowly turned to look, and saw the figure walk into the red brick wall.

Why did he call it 'malevolent' I asked? He screwed up his face and said that something in him just knew it was nasty. He has always wondered if someone was killed there. Of course, the apparition was in daylight, too: and it was spring time. There was plenty of light. Who ever said that spirits only walk at night? Only the writers of cheap tales and creators of myths.

Old Pool, Shepley

First, there was this phone call, late at night and out of the blue, although I had advertised in the Yorkshire papers for uncanny experiences. The voice was shaky; it was an elderly man. The voice down the wire was faint, but the narrative came across to me with a good pace and a high sense of drama.

He had been working in Shepley, many years ago, and remembers something that he has only ever told his wife, as he thought 'blokes would laugh at me if I told'. But he is sure that this happened. The only other man to have seen the thing is now dead, and had never spoken of it.

It was a summer day, and he had been working doing some industrial cleaning; he was stopping for lunch by a pool. He stretched out and snoozed a while, and remembers a dream about a man with a very pale skin, as if the face were diseased. Then he woke up, got hold of his drink and sat forward, looking down at the fish in the pond. But the white face of the dream was there, reflected in the water and obviously belonging to a figure standing behind him. He instinctively called for his workmate, Brian. But Brian was a hundred yards away.

He jumped up and turned around, only to see nothing but the grass. He says he thought this was imagined, after the dream. But a week or so later, he was scrubbing with an iron brush when he heard Brian scream. He ran towards the old back yard where the pond was, and saw Brian standing next to a figure of a man wearing a black gown, like a monk.

'God, it was real as you or me,' Brian had said.

It was described as a white face, pock-marked and grinning. The figure hugged a black coat to itself, as if freezing. It was mostly the thought that 'Brian and me liked a pint… if you get my drift,' that the tale had not been told before this phone call.

Station Hotel, Knaresborough

This lovely old hotel was closed and converted into flats a few years ago, but its bottle green interior and 1960s posters provide fond memories for Jason Gibson, who was manager there at one time. Not so fond , though, are his memories of some disturbing events there. There was a Blue Room and a Yellow Room, and the Blue Room was haunted by an old soldier who used to tap on the floor and walk onto the landing. Jason took some photos of where the man had been seen: one did not come out at all.

Even worse were the activities of the juke box. The object was in the habit of playing discs that were not in the display case; on some occasions it played when there was no plug in the wall socket, and at times, the record played would be Black Sabbath's *Paranoid* – again, a record not in the stock list. Jason spoke to the box supplier to check if there might be another power source other than the mains, and there was none.

Sometimes the cooling fans for the beer had packed up, and the electrics had tripped; but on investigation down in the cellar, something or someone had moved a box across in front of the fuse-box to prevent access. The cooling fan had also been placed on top of a beer-barrel.

There was something nasty in the place, for sure. One Saturday lunchtime, a customer, Mick Abel, was there with his Alsation, and the

Knaresborough, showing the 'dropping well':
Mother Shipton is not the only paranormal story here.

dog just stood up in fear, with all its hair on end. There was an ice-cold patch in that same bar.

Maybe some of the explanation lies in the story of a young girl who was murdered there in 1966; this was in what became a private lounge downstairs. A former resident couple had tried redecorating the room, but there was still something unpleasant in the atmosphere. Jason says that before the body of the girl was found, one of the hotel's regulars had died. It seems that the girl was a babysitter; her body was found in the old church vaults.

Something still persisted as a bad presence there when the former landlord and landlady were in occupancy, before Jason's time: the woman collected crystals, and these kept disappearing without explanation; by the time she left, every single crystal in her collection had mysteriously vanished. Sometimes, people walked into a room to find the three-piece suite shifted and jammed up against a wall.

Even Jason's very last memory of the old Station Hotel is odd: when friends came to collect him, they sensed a weird atmosphere. He had just turned everything off and locked the door, and then everyone noticed that all the lights were turned on. 'It was like watching Celebrity

Squares,' Jason says laconically.

As to why so many unwholesome things have happened there, no-one seems to have an explanation. But the only sure fact is that a murder took place there, and there will be restless spirits about, with an atmosphere of evil. Maybe ripping the place down was the only way to erase the malevolence.

Walton Hall Haunting

Figures seen only as partially complete, such as the Roman soldiers' torsos seen in York at cellar level, proved to be scarce in the tales given by contributors to this work, but one exception is the half-body seen at Walton Hall, near Wakefield. Jan's family have reported seeing such a figure – a woman – before the place was converted into a hotel. At the time of the sighting, it was seen by a pool, and no explanation has ever been given.

But the apparition certainly unnerved Jan's mother when she saw it. The only way to deal with such a thing is laugh it off, as she does, with 'it's only half a tale I'm telling you!'

Factory Floor Poltergeist

The crossroads at the end of Beeston, by Tommy Wass's pub and the road over to Middleton, has always been one of the busiest parts of Leeds. Dewsbury Road generally has enough stories connected with it to make a book of anecdotes sufficient to make anyone believe that it has never been a safe place. A typical example of this is one day when a double-decker bus crossed a junction, as a van with a ladder protruding several feet over the cab also arrived at the junction. The ladder clattered along each window seat of the upstairs and havoc was done: it was commuter time, as well.

But that was man–made mayhem. There was also a certain engineering factory on the road at the far end, and many workers from the milling shop have stories to tell of a noisy spirit. Imagine a quiet lunchtime in summer back in the Swinging Sixties. Most of the workers are outside enjoying a sandwich and a chinwag on the roadside in the sun. Inside, the usually noisy and busy factory floor, crammed with huge milling and turning machines is silent. No tools are being used; no foremen patrol; no office worker walks the aisles to deliver wage packets. But is it so quiet? A man recalls the day when he had slightly injured himself and was seeing the nurse in her small room next to the ground floor. As he came out and walked up an aisle he swears he saw a file leap in the air and hit his leg. 'I wasn't hurt at all,' he says. But it was the shock.

Machine parts used to loosen at times, untouched, and fall to the workbench. Another story was of a steel rule that slapped against a wall. Could there be anything to account for this? One worker remembers that there were some serious injuries there, and on one occasion he saw a young man screaming and running across the floor with blood seeping from his boot. He had just been acting the fool with some tools upstairs, but maybe one of these rough games sent someone to the next world?

The answer will probably never be known. A poltergeist, of course, is reckoned to feed off the energy of the living, notably young people. There were plenty of young men working there at that time. But the explanation seems too trite. Whatever stands on that spot now may still be troubled by mysterious sounds, especially at noon.

Dean Clough Suicide

The massive and impressive sight of Dean Clough mills in Halifax, seen from the North Bridge, was surely one of the wonders of the Victorian landscape around West Yorkshire. It still is a marvellous sight, in the valley between Boothtown and Ovenden. As you drive on the road towards Boothtown the road passes an old stabling area and a sharp turn to the mills and then you find yourself on the old iron bridge. That place has a long history of hauntings, and there may be a source for these.

One night a young man was walking home after a night out, and although it was late, he had taken very little alcohol. It was October and there was a cold breeze across the valley, but with his head down and hands in pockets, he was walking briskly home, having no cash for a taxi and the last bus had gone. He reported later that as he was mid-way over, where the stream lay beneath, he saw a man leaning on the side and looked up to have a full view.

'I thought I heard him say he could see angels and devils,' the young man said.

I investigated the history of the bridge and discovered that there had

*Dean Clough Mills, Halifax. Numerous apparitions have been seen here,
and it featured in a* Derek Acorah's Ghost Towns *programme.*

been one particular suicide there, far back in 1878. I also discovered that
several people had seen the figure and most said that they thought he
was talking to himself.

The newspaper accounts tell the tale of one Benjamin Dowse, who
was a worker at Crossley's at the time; he was living in Victoria Street,
Haley Hill, which is just over on the Bradford side of the mills, just a
short way from the bridge. He had been mentally and physically ill and
had been off work for some time. One local chemist said that Dowse was
suffering from congestion of the lungs.

The poor man had been having hallucinations, complaining of a
numbness at the top of his skull. But surprisingly, he was a teetotaller
and had taken a dislike to beer. He took a long time to die, and in the
Halifax infirmary, he said to his wife, from his death-bed, 'I couldn't help
it... it's because of all that studying.'

His dying was very painful; he had fractured his right thigh and his
face was severely injured. The verdict returned was 'suicide while in a

state of temporary insanity.' Still today, the North Bridge looks attractive beneath the massive and functional concrete of the modern road structures. But it has its ghosts within its arches and supports; its expanse has been trodden by a number of restless spirits, distracted souls, ground down by the satanic mills of the time. Poor Benjamin Dowse was one of those, and the late-night walker may well have met Dowse's unquiet soul that autumn night.

Ye Olde English Gentleman, Hull

Of all the pubs in Yorkshire, this is one that has to be a candidate for a visit from the *Most Haunted* team on Living TV. There are other local pubs with regular and disturbing visitors from beyond, such as the Black Boy on High Street and the Charterhouse near to Drypool Bridge, but regulars report all kinds of paranormal happenings at Ye Olde English Gentleman. The pub is close to the Hull New Theatre and so naturally there are tales of thespians associated with the place. It has another name, the Four in Hand and was previously called the Four Alls, a phrase referring to an old saying: 'I pay for all, I pray for all, I drink for all and I fight for all.'

Stories of unearthly events abound regarding this old pub. One report was of a woman drinking in company, not alone and certainly not even in semi-darkness, and she talked of being pinched in a private place. Staff talk about being shoved or pushed and objects have been known to fly onto the floor from table-tops.

Boggart Hill

All across the county, places with the word 'boggart' may sometimes be seen. Behind those apparently harmless, everyday street names there are some dark tales. A boggart can be a word applied to various manifestations, but usually in Yorkshire the word denotes the entity known to mediums as those spirits which are not grounded in one place but visit and haunt, often with malevolence. Witnesses from the past have used the word to describe sightings of human-like shapes, at first glance merely people moving around normally but then, on closer inspection, their appearance has been monstrous and grotesque.

Boggart Hill Road, Leeds. The name matches the paranormal activity.

In folklore, boggarts have been described as those spectres that tend to return to places of pain and suffering; where, in earlier barbaric times, a person has been tortured or been subject to prolonged suffering, the emanation may be that physical manifestation of the inner torture they had endured.

In north Leeds, on the Seacroft estate, there is Boggart Hill Drive, and a surrounding cluster of Boggart Hill streets. Recent sightings are thin on the ground, but in the 1960s there was apparently a series of uncanny events on that hill. Several people reported seeing, on autumn evenings as they walked down there to catch buses after a day's work at the factories and offices higher up the hill, a figure behind them, coming towards them, forcing them to turn and look.

41

One man recalls that he was working then as a junior clerk and on one occasion, after working late, he was coming down that hill with a workmate. They decided to have a race to the bus-stop. The man sped ahead, then stopped, out of breath, and turned to look for his friend. For a few seconds, he saw no sign of his friend, but instead, a solid, hunched figure, apparently wearing a hooded coat.

'I turned, and saw this shape coming towards me. It was like a man, bent forward, hands in pockets (so I thought) but then as it came near I saw that its face was half pig and half man. For a second, I was speechless, then I heard my friend calling me from behind. He had stopped to have a smoke.'

He shouted for his friend to come and the shape disappeared, but he recalls a strong smell. 'It was like that stink you get when an animal has been in a confined space for too long... a fug, enough to make you retch.'

Another experience was by a woman cleaner, out early in the morning. 'It was bitter cold' she recalls, 'I was wrapped up, a scarf around my head and a big coat. I sort of squinted to look ahead, it was so cold. I could see my breath in front of me. Then I could also see something else. It must have been about half past six, very little light – I saw this thing. It reminded me of that film, the *Hunchback of Notre Dame*. I mean it was an ugly face. He looked at me – well, *it* looked; I can't say it was a man – as if it hated me. Then it made this unearthly noise like a thing in pain, and turned aside to walk into a garden. I crossed the road, staring across all the time, but I could see nothing.'

GUYTRASH

The folklore around dogs has a long history – maybe as old as man himself. In many of the world's major cultures, dogs figure prominently in superstitions. In Egypt, the dog was a sacred being linked to Anubis, and that god was depicted as a dog. In the Vedas, the god of the dead, Yama, has two messenger-dogs who are very fierce. Obviously, they appear in hunting myths and stories. But there is something about the guytrash, otherwise called Black Shuck or the barghest, that challenges the imagination.

Rowland Cooper notes that the accounts of the black dog go back as far as 856 AD when a huge black dog walked into a church service. It ran around the altar before disappearing. This was a story written by Bertin in his *Annales Francorum Regum*.

You can imagine that the priest couldn't compete with that for sheer audience interest.

Sometimes, the local lore has a definite explanation for the appearance of ghostly dogs, as in the barghest : death is certain to be foreshadowed, they say, if he is seen. But one thing is certain: sightings of black dogs have been general in the British Isles. The general description is that they are large and dark, the size of a pony, perhaps. Some accounts talk of it being 'big as a little-ish bear, and yellow, with great eyes like saucers' as Alistair MacGregor reports in *The Ghost Book* (see bibliography).

In 1881 there was an account of man in the Dales meeting such a beast; he was found by a shepherd and the report was that whatever killed him was not mortal. This was at Trollers Gill, not far from Appletreewick. But there are stories from the West Riding, and some of them very recent.

Sometimes in the myths and legends, phantom dogs are in packs, and that is the case with the Gabriel Hounds, told in this section. Some commentators actually go so far as to suggest that the devil takes canine form at times; the writer, Rider Haggard, said this of the Black Dog of Bungay, near Ditchingham, where he lived. But in most cases, the guytrash is silent, menacing and somehow a potential shape-changer, maybe similar in conception to the idea of the witch's 'familiar'.

But don't think that the black dog or shuck is confined to the Broad Acres: Sean McNeaney has researched nine cluster sites of sightings in Lincolnshire alone; there is a particularly rich area for sightings in the Isle of Axeholme and around Gainsborough. The same applies in Yorkshire: some areas seem to have more frequent occurrences than others. The Dales around Sedbergh are a 'hot spot' in this respect, and also Howarth and its immediate locale. But it will come as no surprise to learn that the textile towns have their share.

The knowledge of the guytrash we have is not always necessarily from visions and encounters in the dusk or even sounds of the creatures; there have been cases in which farmers have dug up bones of something they thought to be an ox or a horse, only to discover, on closer inspection, that they were dealing with something having canine teeth – very large ones.

Brackenhill Park Hound

One winter night I answered a phone call, and a Bradford man, Robert Collins, told me about an amazing encounter with a guytrash. He was walking through a part of Brackenhill Park in Bradford, a place where there have been reports of a ghostly lady in black. But this evening walk was to throw up something far more sinister.

It was New Year's Eve, 2002, and he was sitting at home with two friends; they fancied a stroll. His son had some new roller-blades, and joined them; it was around nine thirty. The park has several interesting features, including old springs and wells, at the top end and to the sides. So there is some historical interest in the place.

As Robert walked behind the others, he felt a presence near him. When he turned to one side he saw a dog. He glanced, then turned away for a second, not realising the striking nature of what he had just seen. When he looked again, he saw that it was about three yards long, and the height of a cow. It was silent, and walked across in front of all of the party. His son was the only one to see it at first, until someone called out.

But there was no sense of fear, Robert notes. One of his fellow walkers said, 'If that's a dog I'm blowed!' They made their way back home, and their sighting had not fully sunk in. They purposely walked the path that the beast had taken. They all agreed it was of great size, but moving quietly, with just the sound of breathing.

Robert knows a story about the park, and the place where he saw the beast. Both he and his sister had had the same dream, about a woman in black who exuded a sense of pure evil. In the dream, they had seen a figure attacking his sister's friend with a knife. Only after the encounter with the dog did they realise that the spot it walked on was the place in the dream where the attack took place.

A friend, Jeff, also talked of his experience of seeing a woman in black in the park. But he says that he fell over a fence and saw a woman standing over him. She said something prophetic to him: 'Don't worry about your son.' She had a child with her, and she added, 'I'll look after him.'

Two people in white have also been seen on the stone stairway into the park. But it's mostly been the lady in black – and whether there is any link between her and the guytrash remains unclear. Robert can only add that he has been told there is a ley line from Beacon Hill, and that he has read about a guytrash haunting Thornton, just down the road, in years gone by.

Roundhay Park Guytrash

Close to Roundhay Park, the green stretch of Soldiers' Field, north Leeds, is a happy place in the daylight. On a Sunday there will be football matches there, and people walking their dogs. But we have to wonder whether those dogs can sense any evil, for the well-kept fields are a different place in the dark. It was here that the Yorkshire Ripper struck in his early days, killing one of his victims there in 1977. But there are other bothersome spirits around this area, including a dog of giant size.

He has been seen both on the fields and further up, on the approach to the park. At least two people have seen his outline at dusk, one while jogging and another walking to a restaurant in the early evening. The Roundhay or Oakwood guytrash is black, dull-coated, and as big as a donkey. His eyes are reputedly red and he is said to appear when a person is so troubled that he comes to shadow their foreboding of decline. If you see him, then it is a warning to rethink, to gather your reason. A jogger was just starting to tire when he saw the dog. 'I felt my lungs rasping and I thought that's enough for one session. Then I felt something by my side…' He hadn't drunk anything intoxicating, and swears that people would ridicule him if he told them, but he saw what he thought was a wild pony at first.

'But it was like a Labrador, only much bigger, and it snorted…'

If it was a faery dog, then Scots folk would say it was a transmuted goblin, portending death; but in Yorkshire we tend to have changed the view and talk more of a warning, like a shadow falling over a lawn at noon, to make you shiver.

Dog on the Moor, Lindley

Walkers heading out towards the Pennines have given testimony to meetings with a guytrash en route to Saddleworth moors from the north west of Huddersfield. The walk is long and tiring if done in full; the start is off the Halifax road, and follows a steady incline, luckily with several inns along the way.

Locals rarely seem to know of it; and there appear to be no folkloric records. The people who did put on record the sight and sounds of an unearthly hound make it seem reminiscent of the hound said to roam Haworth Moor: seen only fleetingly but heard baying and apparently close by.

This has to be said because the Lindley hound has been heard more often than seen. One man told me that he knows the sound of a real dog from the sound he heard one quiet Sunday night as he was walking back home towards Paddock, tasting the welcome pint waiting for him, and lapping up the peace, when he heard from behind something 'like you imagine from the Baskervilles.' Did he see anything? He turned and stood 'stock still, taking a steady look up there.' He thought for a second that he saw a shape, moving almost like a large cat, but the frame was canine, the stance and mien like that of a dog.

Up on Saddleworth itself in years gone by, poachers have recorded sightings of guytrash. The most abiding memory is of the red eyes. As recently as the 1960s, there was an account of a dog 'the size of a hoss' and with eyes that pierced you, up on Saddleworth. The guytrash or shuck in some myths is a dog that follows you, portending death much the same as the hearing of the screech-owl at night. My friend who reported the sighting knew of this superstition, and notes that he 'Didn't give it time to follow him, just in case.'

Kirkby Overblow Black Shuck

This is the one guytrash tale that accounts for the animal as a neglected sheep-dog, and the creature is supposed to visit Kirkby. The story is that a farmer in the area left his dog guarding some sheep in an isolated spot, and completely forgot that he had done so. Tradition has it that the dog eventually came home and battled to be let in at his home, but was not heard, even though he scratched and scraped the wood. But he was feeble with lack of food and had not the strength to be heard.

He went back into the wild to die, starved to his end. Is he the ghostly dog of the village? It all stems from the inconceivable fact that a man would ever do such a thing ; no doubt, if the creature menacing the highway is the spirit of the dog, then some might have felt that the man deserved such fearful haunting.

Dog myths often relate to stories like this, with a human centre and a community with a genuine affection for their animals; hence, a death through neglect is something horrendous, and likely to echo through the boundaries of life and death.

In this case, maybe imagination transformed a dog actually known and recorded as being alive into something mythic: but in the end, there is no difference in the origins of phenomena when we try to account for appearances. The actual experience is all that matters to the person who sees something paranormal. Science can look for answers. There were for instance, frequent reports of mad dogs on the loose in Yorkshire, reported in the pages of the *Leeds Mercury* at the end of the eighteenth century. It would be easy – too easy – to see this as the cause of 'imagined' spectral hounds.

The Gabriel Hounds, Mankinholes

With this legend, we enter the realm of folklore, and the dogs in a pack, with huntsman in attendance. This gang are supposedly seen tearing down the Bride Stones gorge, and then disappearing in Mankinholes. As with all such similar tales across the land, they are reported to scream in such a disturbing manner that they attain the status of a foreboding of imminent death for any person who is unfortunate enough to hear the piercing yell.

The Gabriel pack are similar to the accounts of the Black Shuck seen in packs on Shap Fell, in the Lakes; what they have in common is the fearsome late-night terror of the sight preceding the inevitable deathly sound. This version is unlike any other reported guytrash sighting, as the more normal pattern is for the creature to slink quietly, accompanying a lone traveller in menacing silence.

Mankinholes in this respect has the resonance of the petrifying vision of Herne the Hunter or the hounds of Odin in the Germanic and Celtic myths. But the Yorkshire ones are 'Gabriel' hounds from the story of the Angel of Death, who was supposed to be the only angel who could speak Syriac, and the extension of the horrible haunting noise made is with the 'hounds' being called 'Gabble ratchet' or wild geese, as the noise of a massive flock of geese has a similar sound to that of hounds. Legend says that this sound is made by the souls of unbaptised children.

These children are condemned to run and moan until the Day of Judgement. If that is the sound heard at Mankinholes, then God help anyone nearby.

Haworth Guytrash

Many writers have noted the fact that Haworth people in years gone by felt that there was a guytrash abroad in the streets of the village. Charlotte Brontë talked about the great spectral hound being 'a lion-like creature with long hair and a huge head.' In chapter twelve of *Jane Eyre* we have mention of the creature, and scholars say that Charlotte took more from the Lancashire sources than the Yorkshire ones, as in the folklore records of 1890, when it was known as 'skriker' – in other words, the foreboding of death if it looks you in the eye.

In other words, it is an omen, and Charlotte believed in omens. The village superstitions and anecdotes of encounters with the dog were extant in her time, and indeed there have been a few more recent ones. The most striking and mysterious is surely that huge long-haired dog seen as a threatening shadow by a walker returning home from Top Withins a bit later than planned. The man who tells the tale was not young, and he admits that his eyesight is not what it was, 'but the thing was following me… I saw it first in the heather, then in a hollow… below me as I took a path across towards Stanbury…'

He was a seasoned walker and fit enough to move very sharply towards the lights of the houses and pubs in Stanbury, but he says he had read of the ghosts around that part of the Haworth area, including that of Emily Brontë, but 'the last thing I expected was a damn girt dog!'

Some say the guytrash of Haworth is just an extension of the imagination in a place where tourists want desperately to find the mystical elements in the Brontë story. Just try telling that to my walker friend. He won't go back that way again, ever.

'A Dog or a Bear' in a Churwell Yard

If you don't know the area, then let me tell you that the village of Churwell lies just off the Leeds to Morley road, between a viaduct and the memorial garden at the top of the hill. If you visit the place now you will see housing developments where once there were open fields. There will be nothing remarkable to distinguish this corner of Yorkshire from many others. Yet not too long ago, the village was a mix of red-brick terraces and dark courts, together with newer houses on the Morley side, and farmlands to the south towards Gildersome.

In old Churwell, on the side of a cobbled lane called Low Fold, there stood a white farmhouse; the family there kept pigs and hens, and their smallholding bordered on a large farm, so there was open land behind. But squat in the middle of this, in a garth behind the cottage was a shadowy, ancient spot known for its bad atmosphere. The memories I have gathered are about a time when life in Yorkshire villages was primitive by modern standards: the family on Low Fold had no inside toilet. They had simply an outside 'midden' round the back in the garth, shared between themselves and two other families.

This story took place almost sixty years ago, and it is hard to believe that this account is the only one of such a disturbing encounter. It has all the ingredients of a traditional ghost story: dark night, a person alone, and peaceful normality being shattered by a stealthy intrusion of something uncanny.

Of all the tales collected for this book, none is so harrowing as the beast of Low Fold. One person who used to live there told me of the time she went out to the midden on a winter's night. In those days, she says, 'You took some newspaper with you… we were short of cash…' She was shivering behind the flaky, fragile door, and all was quiet. But she became aware of a shadow. In a shaky voice she drummed up the courage to ask, 'Is anyone there?' Her brother had been known to play tricks on her so she shouted his name and was 'right mad at him' but there was no reply. Then she heard a deep sound like something huge snorting, like a large horse.

'It was maybe a shire horse by the sound of it...' she recalls. But when outside, walking back home and imagining ghosts in every shadowy corner, she knows that she became aware of a massive animal, only half real, not fully substantial. It was more like a dog than anything else, but could have been 'a dog or a bear'.

The area where the creature appeared was enclosed by a high wall, and there were no real street lights at the time. The woman simply could not cry for help – it was a run of sheer panic. It was always a daft idea to run on the cobbles as well, 'most of us bairns had cut knees from that...'

'I ran. Ran like the wind... never screamed nor nowt... But I told my dad. He laughed it off...' But she will never forget the terror. Old Churwell appears to have been a peculiarly active location for spiritual energies or even visitations; others have reported a figure of a woman in the back yards near where the village general store once stood. Many spoke of a man pulling a barrow of wood sticks, a figure they never felt sure was actually there in reality.

None of this is apparent now in commuterland, as the village expands around the old school. But somewhere back in folk memory there are sprites and spectres lingering around the village.

Hound in the Woods, Keighley

We end this survey of spectral hounds with a case of an opposite, totally odd reason for the apparition – to protect a person rather than portend danger or death.

Rowland Cooper tells of a strange confrontation with a Black Dog way back in 1893 in some woods near Keighley. This was actually written for the record books of the Wesleyan Methodist Church. A certain Mr Reynard was walking home from a committee meeting when he walked into some woods. It was a terrible mistake to walk alone in that black place.

For Mr Reynard felt the sensation of being touched by something or someone, and when he looked, he saw, quite clearly, a large black dog. A short way further on he saw two men approaching, and as they neared them the dog growled. Finally, as Reynard emerged from the wood and came to a lamp, he looked to check on the beast and found that it had gone. This was near the Old Toll Bar. He pressed on, and was later home than expected.

But the amazing outcome of the encounter was that his wife told him that a neighbour had called to see her and was anxious that Mr Reynard might be walking on a route on which his son had been attacked by two men. It appears that the guytrash may be benign after all, at least in Keighley.

To sum up, the guytrash in the West Riding has, in most sightings, been similar to the commonest sounds and visions of the shuck or barguest in other counties. The general nature of the experience is one of fearsome foreboding. But there is a variety of types: the figure is not always black, and not necessarily a 'skriker' as the screech owl myth is. Of all the manifestations of spectres on record, the guytrash is the one with perhaps the most threat, terror and disturbance, notably when the 'pack' of hounds is allegedly seen.

Most folklorists would seem to agree that the origins of these sightings may well lie in the uneasy duality of the dog itself: brother to the wolf yet also 'man's best friend'. The wild elements, as in 'wolf-man' stories, will always be with us in film and fiction, but people usually have a peculiarly blank disbelief when the subject of the guytrash is brought up. I recently asked a broadcaster and naturalist about his opinion on this. He had never heard of any sightings in his county (Lincolnshire) and could only rest on old tales and drunken imaginings.

Yet there is something in the guytrash that twists and distorts the familiar canine image and his relationship with man. I was once told of a black dog seen slinking along a street in a village near Selby – huge, padding the earth, having no connection with any particular human: just being an accompanying figure on the man's walk.

Ghosthunter Alasdair MacGregor has said that he heard the phrase 'black dog' used more loosely, by his landlady, who said, 'Yer gey crotchety the day ma laddie! I see the Black Dog's on yer back!' In other words, part of the answer may lie in our affection for the Jekyll and Hyde paradox about ourselves, and that the guytrash is some manifestation of our own darker side.

HISTORICAL HAUNTINGS

The West Riding has almost too many villas, mansions, halls and municipal buildings for the paranormal investigator to cope with. In addition to the celebrated places such as Temple Newsam, a traveller is likely to turn a corner in any one of the clusters of small towns in the West Riding conurbations, to discover a grand old place built to order by one of the nouveaux riches of the Victorian and Edwardian periods. It comes as no surprise to learn that very few of these places are free of any alleged haunting. In buildings with a long pedigree and plenty of oak beams, we tend to imagine things perhaps.

But there is nothing simply imagined in the following accounts. In most cases there have been far too many recorded sightings of inexplicable phantoms or disturbing sounds emanating from corners and galleries quite deserted at the time. Places where there have been generations of residents naturally have human stories, and many investigators think that walls collect and retain the electrical impulses of life and even speech. The line of thought suggests that somehow the fabric of buildings collects and holds a packed stack of layers, time-records, like rings on a tree-trunk.

Shibden Hall Visitor

We could easily make this plural and say 'visitors', as the ghost of a young girl drowned has been seen nearby, and tobacco smoke lingers at times in some parts. But the most thoroughly noted and monitored spirit walking the beautiful rooms of Shibden is most probably Anne Walker, lover of Anne Lister, the nineteenth century writer and traveller. The hall is an ancient place, but to the eye appears to be largely a Tudor building, although there is a firm presence of the Augustan Age, as Lord Lonsdale was the principal owner in the eighteenth century, and visitors cannot fail to be impressed by the handsome coach he had made, decked in his bright yellow livery.

But famously, it is the red room which has the echoes and manifestation of poor Anne Walker's restless shade; here she barricaded herself in, under the stresses of mental illness, and attempted suicide. A constable was called and when he came to investigate and finally entered the room, he found her in a terrible state, with lots of her blood spilled, and masses of smelly, uneaten food.

Not only Anne's tragic tale, with the end coming in her incarceration in an asylum, but the general air of violence, threat and unease is often in the air when we read Anne Lister's diaries. She talks of groups of men outside in the dark, clearly up to no good, and sometimes with firearms. They were violent and uncertain times, and it seems that even Anne Lister herself was doomed to a sad decline, dying of the plague in Russia.

Overall, Shibden's position and vistas suggest the typically atmospheric historical site: the surrounding fields and even the lawns and gardens, appear to have something permanently there which is meant to create unease. In recent times, visitors have reported more than simply the smell of tobacco (apparently that relates to John Lister, last of the line, who was rarely found without a pipe in his mouth): the figure of a young woman has been seen on a few occasions. Clearly, something about the oak-framed windows and tall chimneys makes the environment into a stately but shady version of Yorkshire Gothic, and if you like to put yourself at the disposal of the Other World beyond this, then go to Shibden at dusk.

East Riddlesden Hall

Keighley's most notable haunted building has the perhaps questionable record of its haunting by the Grey Lady – a photograph. But the image is described in one reproduction as 'a photographer's idea of the ghostly lady…' This ploy is surely never advisable, when there are already far too many carefully fabricated ruses and scams in the world of paranormal investigation. But in spite of this, East Riddlesden Hall has a dreadful story attached to its history.

There have been apparent sightings of several ghosts here, in a spot with a long history (built in 1692), but the Grey Lady takes centre stage. Her tale is that she was found at home with her lover one day by her husband. The story is that she was locked away and the boyfriend bricked up in the building. This was barbaric, of course, but we need to remember that even in the mid eighteenth century, there was a case in York of a wife being burned alive for the murder of her husband.

The Grey Lady is seen walking up the stairs. In former times, a housekeeper often reported seeing the figure, and addressed the spectre, never to receive a reply. More recent residents have heard creakings up above, and a voice from nowhere has spoken to people, usually wishing them goodnight.

More mysterious is the White Lady, and her story bears a close resemblance to one notable Welsh haunting, in Nanteos House in Dyfed: the lady had been hunting, and at the end of the day, only her horse returned home. The desperate search achieved nothing and she was never found. Is she in the lake? Nanteos was similar, only the young lady's spirit has been seen in the stables and in the grounds. At East Riddlesden, in recent times, visitors have noted parts of the land which do not seem 'inviting' for the living to walk, even in daylight.

Blue Lady, Temple Newsam

In the case of this most famous haunted site in and around Leeds, I have personal experience of the Blue Lady, a woman from the celebrated Ingram family, who has often been seen. I was walking along a gallery between two rooms in the mansion when I felt drawn to look at one particular spot by a wall. I stared, feeling increasingly nervous but not knowing why. As I looked, a chair moved and I heard a sound as of a stiff fabric brushing against wood. This was in the daytime; I had heard of the Blue Lady, and assumed this was her.

Temple Newsam is a magnificent place, with a majestic setting, to the north east of Leeds, not far from the Selby Road and Garforth. Its Elizabethan rooms and architecture make it totally compelling as a visual spectacle, and in summer evenings not long ago there were several *son et lumieres* performances in the grounds. A Mr Longfellow recorded a strange experience on one of these occasions. He was sitting to the side, away from the main crowd, and found himself being compelled to turn around. 'It was as if someone was calling me' he says. After a few minutes, he lost all interest in the light show and sensed a whisper behind him. When he turned around he saw a woman dressed in a long white dress, walking into the shadows about thirty feet away.

My correspondent asked a few questions and read up on the place afterwards, and learned of the other much-documented female presence at the mansion: the White Lady. This was Lady Jane Dudley, who was besotted with the ill-fated Lord Darnley, sent to woo and wed Mary Queen of Scots by the Virgin Queen. Poor Lady Jane, unable to have the man she loved, hanged herself with her girdle: this was, again, a tragedy occurring actually within the walls, in her own room.

Such encounters are not unusual at Temple Newsam. Here all kinds of dynamics from past historical events are evident. There was even a murder there: a servant called William Collinson killed Phoebe Gray, a maid. This was early in the eighteenth century and, of course, Collinson was hanged at York Castle.

As to the Blue Lady herself: she was one of the Ingram family in ownership of the mansion in the mid seventeenth century. She was set upon by robbers while travelling one day, and was most likely not only robbed but physically wounded by her assailants, because sightings of her spectre have all had one detail in common – a scar near her right eye. One of the most vivid witnesses to her visitations has been noted by Andy Owens, who writes that in 1926 a visitor saw the figure of a woman in Carolean dress, with this distinctive scar. This man had no foreknowledge of the Blue Lady.

There are those who put everything down to the Knights Templars, who were the original founders of the place. The continuing mystique and myth attached to this order sometimes makes them sound like a brotherhood akin to the Mafia. But certainly, as several other places in Britain active with spiritual manifestations have links with the Templars, who knows how much substance there may be in this? For instance, a notoriously haunted and dangerous bend on the A road from Lincoln to Sleaford is close to a Templar site.

Whatever the truth, the myths surrounding Temple Newsam will never take over from the ongoing sightings by ordinary people visiting this wonderfully rich and appealing historically important aristocratic home.

Piece Hall Handprints

The grand and imposing Piece Hall in the centre of Halifax is the kind of place that one would expect to find a resident ghost. The colonnades around the central square have many shadowy corners, and the Georgian grandness of the stone suggests something for the nobility, not for every-day trade. But such it was: the hub of the textile trade, where pieces of cloth were brought to be sold, from the many weavers' cottages around the local valleys.

One interesting sight is full of intrigue, though: a pair of hand prints on the stonework by the Westgate entrance. Thirty years ago, the main legend about the hands was that these were from the hands of a murderer who was caught trying to scale the walls, and as they were a killer's prints, they would be there forever. It would be fun to take this kind of reading and let the myth persist, but a note was recently found, dating from the year 1890 that states the far more probable origin of the marks: a young man was acting the goat with friends, using some of the substances left by cleaners, and he dipped his hands into some acid.

There does seem to be a ghost in the Piece Hall, however: a little girl from the nineteenth century when there was a workhouse nearby. She visits one of the small shops on the upper storey galleries: a mineral and jewellery business. Some say she is called Mary, and her footsteps have been heard, along with whispers and laughing. We would surely like to believe that a workhouse girl from those times could be happy sometimes.

Wainhouse Tower

There is something fey about the Wainhouse Tower, a folly not far from the busy road junction at the end of King Cross, Halifax. Walking past towards Savile Park, one has the feeling that the place has secrets, and sometimes visitors from the world of the dead.

The tower was originally a place with a function: to extract smoke from the dyeworks nearby, with the use of a flue between them. The Gothic structure also failed to fulfil its second intended use: as a well-situated observatory. But a telescope could not be made to fit in the space available. It has even been a henhouse.

But there have been accounts of a ghost of a young girl, some given to me directly from local people. It seems that in the Second World War, a G.I. was beaten up for having a liaison with a Halifax woman. Something about the Savile Park and King Cross area attracts malicious doings. There was a murder done by a Canadian soldier only a few hundred yards from the tower, and of course, about the same distance away, Peter Sutcliffe, the Yorkshire Ripper, struck one night.

In this case, the young woman involved was distraught by the violence and punishment. Some accounts say that she was followed by the eventual attackers, as she went to meet the soldier. If she actually had to stand and watch the vicious assault, then it would scar the girl forever, and that was indeed the story. The victim only just recovered from the attack, but her mental trauma went on. She died in a mental hospital in 1974.

She has been seen weeping by the tower, and some had heard her utter the despondent words, 'They done for him...' A local resident told me that quite recently he and his wife have heard a young woman weeping by the roadside, as they walked by on a quiet evening. But as they moved closer to see the cause, nothing or no-one could be seen.

Otley Old Hall and the Planet Ruler

Otley, though so close to Leeds, has a very strong presence of the past; to walk the streets from the car park area today, across towards the Chevin and Queen's Terrace, is to be aware of an array of old stone buildings from long ago, still with a strange moodiness, as if they resent the busy modern town being constructed above and around them.

The streets and ginnels abound with ghost stories. Kirkgate seems to be a focus, and the Old Hall, a Georgian residence originally, has been changed markedly over the years. It used to be in the hands of Thomas Barker, who died in 1773; he was responsible for the growth of the Viscount Halifax dynasty, as his daughter married Charles Woold of Bradford's Bolling Hall (see later in this section).

The ghost here is notably that of an old man. In 1995, the author Harold Walker, told of his own connection with the place, and of the fact that the old man used to sit on a particular chair, looking out in the direction of the Chevin. Harold's sister-in-law Kathleen, lived there for many years and he asked about the ghost. Kathleen said that one thing was for sure – a chair always kept across the room was often found positioned in the bay, where the old man's spirit reputedly sat.

More bizarre is one of the other prominent Otley ghosts: that of Mrs Horner, who was a 'planet ruler', supposed mystic. Harold Walker's grandfather, a printer, was apprenticed to the trade, working for Webb Millington. One time, in the very early hours, he was climbing the stairs to bed when he came face to face with the figure of an old woman, typically wearing one of the distinctive frill caps we see so often in the old photographs of the time. James Walker was in panic and sprinted from the scene. He would not return to that place, ever.

The spectre had to be Mrs Horner; the description was certainly her. She had lived there for sixty years, and was locally quite a celebrity: it was said that on one occasion she broke an egg and spun a sixpence, thus bringing good fortune to her family. According to Harold, it was verified by the future rise of the Walker offspring.

Bolling Hall

Today, Bolling Hall is a museum, standing to the north of Bowling Park, Bradford, and close to Fairfax Community School. There is little to indicate what a troubled past the building has seen, including a most remarkable visitation by a spirit.

Back in the 1850s, one writer talked about the history of Bolling Hall with reference to its former moat and high walls, its deer park and imposing aspect, with tall chimneys and castellations. At that time, the commentators spoke of its provision of 'fresh unadulterated air' for the

Bolling or Bowling Hall, Bradford, where the lady begged pity for Bradford.

58

hard-working local population. History it has in abundance, as the old portraits of national and local worthies prove.

But back in the Civil War years, after the battle of Adwalton Moor where the Roundheads were beaten, the Royalist leader, the Earl of Newcastle, moved into the hall. The second siege of the city was under-way, with brave Sir Thomas Fairfax defending and Newcastle aimed his cannon at the walls. When Fairfax surrendered, it was generally expected that Newcastle would spare no mercy for anyone in the place, and that there would be bloodshed and destruction. But he changed his mind and gave the order that quarter should be shown to the Bradfordians.

Why did he change his mind? The tale is that as he was in bed, the ghost of a white lady appeared before him, pulled back the bedclothes and said, 'Pity poor Bradford...' It may well be that this is merely the essence of something far more radically affecting than such a plain, traditional appari-tion story. An account of this written in the Victorian period suggests that it was a convenient way to explain a change of plan without necessarily having to go into some personal circumstances concerning the Earl.

It all remains shrouded in mystery. But Bolling Hall will have its residual presences, and they will know the secrets. Look out for signs of the white lady when you visit this noble hall, absolutely steeped in a history of turbulence and upheaval, as the old portraits show.

Bridge End, Leeds

A walk down Briggate, past the Calls and towards the bridge over the Aire today will bring you to a row of shops still on the corner of Call Lane and Bridge End. Nothing would lead you to suspect just how much fascinating social history – much of it violent – has taken place there. It has always been a stretch of Leeds with a focus for human activity, some of it on the nefarious side at times. It also has at least two ghostly presences.

A photograph of Bridge End taken in 1870 shows that there was a bottling store there, with a tavern huddled up against it, the pavement lined with barrels. The shop by what would become the post office advertises 'Cordials and Black beer.' All in all, this is a working class drinking place, close to some dark alleys much frequented by ladies of the night.

One of the ghosts may well be the unhappy spirit of Winifred Sharp, who was killed at the post office there in 1966. This is actually an unsolved case, and is likely to remain that way. Several witnesses have spoken of seeing the shape of a woman by the shops, particularly at dusk. One person was certain that someone spoke to them when they were alone in the shop there: a voice asking for 'small change'.

Even more interesting, there has been a spirit there since late Victorian times, and it may well have been caught on camera. A photograph exists of Number 30, a barber's shop in 1869, and next door is a black, unwholesome ginnel leading to a slum court. At a window over the ginnel we have two figures: a woman and a little child. What is particularly interesting for a paranormal investigator is that the face of the adult (most likely a woman) is blurred even in close-up. The blurring is integral to the composition of the image: it cannot be a camera-based distortion.

Steve Jones presents this picture, with comments about the image, in his *Yorkshire: The Sinister Side* (see bibliography) and the reader doesn't need to be a photographic expert to see that there is something insubstantial in the outline. The street and the bridge have always been linked to robbery, drink and prostitution until the mid twentieth century, and violent deaths create restless ghosts. As a young man in the sixties, I used to walk on Bridge End several times every week, walking to work. On one occasion, myself and a friend both turned to answer a voice that was in the shadows, asking us for 'a bob for the bairn...' only to find that the door-frame only contained a bag of old clothes.

Leeds Parish Church and Viaduct

A little triangle of waste ground between Leeds Parish Church and the railway viaduct going over the road by the bus station is a place with an almost tangible malevolence at certain times of day. That patch of grass in days gone by was frequented by drunks and prostitutes. It was notorious for assaults and murders. Circling the area, on all sides of the Parish Church, are a labyrinth of alleys, yards and old public houses. In former and wilder times, it was a dangerous habit to walk through this area late at night.

Today, the spot has been made attractive with seats and flowers; it is well maintained. But over the years c.1960 to 2000 there have been many inexplicable experiences on and around this place. A man who once did some 'courting' down where the arches under the viaduct offer some privacy, told a tale of absolute unease and disquiet. He was holding hands with his girlfrend, and was walking out towards a bus stop, when he says they both felt this irresistible need to stare at a very specific spot – it was towards the rear of a yard opposite the pub. He recalls that it was as if some piercing eyes were staring at them. When they heard what he calls a 'hiss' he squeezed his girl's hand and they both sprinted up Kirkgate to where there was some light.

Leeds Parish Church. Does the tormented spirit of a murdered woman haunt the grass nearby?

Could it be that the murdered souls walk here? Often, apparitions are repeatedly seen or heard in places where the ghost when alive was most happy. This would certainly apply to Mrs Judge, who was bludgeoned to death in this waste land sixty years ago, as I write. She loved the pubs, the company and the sheer life of that part of Leeds between what was the Quarry Hill Flats and the Calls. People said she loved children, and would always stop to talk to them and chuck them under the chin, or give them sweets.

A man who worked as a barkeep in one of the public houses near the Parish Church explained that many of his customers had talked about hearing a voice say something in that 'daft voice you make when you talk to kids.' One man said he had seen a figure of a woman in loud clothes, ill-matched, and gaudy, walking briskly towards the viaduct, and then disappearing into the wall.

The presence of the Parish Church seems to have little benign effect in terms of freeing this area from his ghosts. They clearly find it to be a welcoming place for those who are restless and in their own personal limbo of pain.

Kirkstall Abbey Haunting

Anyone growing up in Leeds cannot fail to be impressed by the position of Kirkstall Abbey: it is nestling in a valley between massive housing estates on the slopes on the Bramley side, and up and across the opposite valley side, taking the walker to Headingley, there is a crammed suburbia of student accommodation and streets, factories and noise. But there Kirkstall stands, proud and beautiful, and has done so since around 1160.

The precincts cover about forty acres; dominating that land for centuries has been a long line of abbots, of all kinds and tastes. From various accounts and memoirs, it appears that the little-known tale of one of these men, a certain John de Thornberg, may well be the rather menacing spirit sometimes sensed in the ruins. Monkish spectres have a special attraction for the writer and the investigator; but in this case, it would appear to be difficult to prove anything conclusive. John and his cronies were thugs: they were the terror of the area in the late fourteenth century. He even attacked the Vicar of Sandal at one point. A servant was killed.

Many visitors have spoken of a figure in monkish gowns and cloak, and have reported a sense of malevolence; John was the type to cling to his stamping ground, even after death. Surely he is the one who stands threateningly, as if to say that no-one belongs there but him. Many years ago, a Leeds man took his family on a picnic in the grounds. Then, thirty years ago, he says that it was different, 'you could take your kids anywhere and let them play...' But this summer Sunday is one he will never forget. His two children came running to him, one of them sweating and hot with shock, saying, 'That man in a long dress, he shouted at us!'

The good father went to investigate. Confusingly, there was a stone which could have been taken for a human shape – in a child's imagination at least. But he says that 'for the rest of the day they fretted. The eldest one talked about the man with the shaggy beard... and a frown...'

Emily Brontë still Walking

Any self-respecting Tyke wants Emily Brontë to live forever. After all, she and her work are one of the crowning glories of Yorkshire achievement. Tourists flock in their thousands to pay homage to her in Haworth.

Many of them walk the moors and experience the 'Brontë Waterfall' or press on to Top Withins and feel sure that they have caught a glimpse of Cathy and Heathcliff on the wild moors. But how many have seen her still walking among the heather? Marie Campbell writes of several locals who have, in recent years, been convinced that Emily is still around the village.

Marie was writing in 2001, and she went into sightings going back to the 1960s. We want to see her ghost, and the lady in white, often seen walking from Stanbury to Top Withins, is exactly who and where we would expect to see her if she were still flitting around in spirit form.

One of the most insistent assertions of her presence there is surely that from the owner of the Toby Jug restaurant whom Marie refers to. He even wrote to the papers to tell of her appearances on eight occasions, always on the anniversary of her death. He even said that he saw her upstairs in his property, 'chuckling.'

A blessing, rather than an exorcism, was eventually performed. Yet still more statements of Emily being seen or heard have come forward. Of course, the whole romantic ethos she embraced is taken on by her followers, and a certain receptivity will always see what it wishes to see if the time is right. But all I can say is that in many visits to the village, and in dozens of walks on the moors, I have never been disappointed in sensing the presence of the past: on one occasion, I did see a figure which was more than likely not substantial and not of this world. This was in fact a dog: a black dog, most decidedly not a guytrash. This creature was slinking across the road by the Black Bull in front of me as I returned from walk to Stanbury. It dissolved into a wall.

Morning Walker at Brighouse

Very few folk would choose to walk the long A 644 from Halifax to Brighouse. Traffic is heavy and it would not be pleasant, but on a stretch of this road we have a case of one of that well-recorded phenomena, the walker on the road. Across Britain there are dozens of these, and the Brighouse one conforms to the pattern. It is usually late in the morning, and often on a Sunday. The driver sees a young man walking on the side of the road, the thumb arched as he hitches a lift.

Then the figure suddenly turns, steps into the road, and in seconds, the driver sees the face and it appears that the next thing will be a deadening thud as the young man is hit and probably crushed. But of course, when the car is stopped and the motorist gets out to look, there is nothing to see. The man who walks has long hair and wears a check shirt. He appears to stare and his mouth gapes as you go closer. A Halifax man told of this experience; it was a Sunday morning and he had been out to do some emergency plumbing. 'I was tired... red-eyed... I could have imagined it all.' He says, trying to laugh. But the truth is he cannot erase the memory. 'Yes, I thought I'd killed a man... my heart was thumping like it was up my throat... then nothing... just nothing...'

These repeat in many places. To my knowledge, the record for similar occurrences on one stretch of road is in North Lincolnshire, between Epworth and Crowle. But maybe readers know different?

Armley Gaol Spirits

The daunting sight of Armley gaol, a place with the grim aspect of a castle, is as terrible as some of the scenes of death which have taken place within its walls. Of all the desperate characters who have met their end there dangling from a rope, Charlie Peace has to be the most notorious. Most Leeds people of the previous two generations know the name; there has even been a children's skipping song about him, with the lines, 'Charlie killed a copper / Charlie came to grief.' He certainly did: a drawing in the *Illustrated Police Gazette* for 1879 shows him standing on the trap-door surrounded by officers and clergy, as the cap is placed over his head. William Marwood, inventor of the more humane 'long drop' officiates.

But did we see the last of Charlie? Officers who have trod the wings at Armley say not. All gaols which formerly held condemned cells surely have a particularly gaunt and uneasy atmosphere. At Armley, it is said that Charlie haunts not only the wing where the cell was, but the administration block as well. People claiming to have seen him in the few square yards where he last walked this earth have noted the protruding jawline and the sunken eyes. Anyone seeing a photograph or drawing of the killer would see those features.

More insistent is a spectre of what may be the soldier who cut the throat of his live-in partner, Annie Mayne. He was hanged by Thomas Pierrepoint in 1919, and the fact that he had served King and country in the trenches did not save him from the noose. Various professionals who have worked there say they have seen the figure of a man in soldier's garb, a 'Tommy Atkins' as some put it.

This could well be Ben Benson. He killed Annie when he came home and found her in bed with another man. At his trial he said how she was a 'Jezebel' and he repeated the word several times. A former inmate swears he heard the word whispered in his ear.

In the barbaric days of the noose, there were some innocent people who died, and some who insisted to the last breath that their execution was unjust. Benson saw his act as a kind of Biblical retributive justice. No wonder, then, that his soul may be yet in purgatory and wandering the wings in Armley. Officers on night shift watch out.

Re-Born in Haworth?

Many writers have told the tale of Nicola Wheater, most recently Trutz Hardo (see bibliography), and the case raises the thorny issues of possession or indeed, reincarnation. Nicola kept telling her mother about when she had 'been a boy' and had a dog called Muff. Her memories of what was beginning to seem like a former life were extremely vivid and authentic: so much so that Mrs Wheater took her daughter to Haworth, where the girl said she had died under a train – in her past life as a boy.

So began one of the most remarkable Yorkshire paranormal tales. The narrative of how Nicola's mother gradually uncovered data that made the tale very likely is a 'modern classic' of the question. Nicola said she had been called Benson formerly, and had taken the family to the place where she had lived in Haworth. Then her mother looked into the records. Various data began to confirm this, most notably the fact that Nicola said her father had been a railway worker: a worker with that occupation, name of Benson, was recorded as having been living at the known address in 1875. Then, although a son, John, had been recorded at the 1881 census, he was missing from the list in the next one, ten years later.

Was Nicola possessed or had she in truth lived before? The entire topic of previous alleged lives was perhaps most famously mediated in the case of the Bloxham tapes, when the psychologist of that name regressed voluntary subjects and they spoke as people who were living somehow in a previous age.

Nicola Wheater's statements and story definitely appear to confirm the fact that, whichever of the two possibilities happened, the results were uncanny. The tale has elements of the familiar 'little playmate' discussed earlier. The only comment that might be of value in achieving some kind of resolution is that, of course, the girl's behaviour never suggested possession to the parents. Other patterns of behaviour might logically have been expected if that were the case.

But a case in my own experience was very similar, and in many ways recalls the pattern: a school friend of mine, back in the 1950s in north Leeds, was always saying, as we played on our estate, that he used to live in a large old house we often passed. It was a massive place, mostly behind high privet hedges, but we would look through the iron gates and he would say how, when he lived there before, he had a parrot and a wooden rocking horse. He even talked about a cleaner called Mrs Lamb. And he said that he died because he choked, struggling to breathe, and that Mrs Lamb had tried to save him.

I told others about this, including my aunt, and she said what I now see was the obvious answer: he was fantasizing and creating a dream-narrative, just as you do when playing with toy soldiers or imagining that the Dark Riders are after you.

But there was just one small nagging doubt about the explanation. He had told me and two others kids who played with us that he used to be called Sam and his father Peter. One day I asked the old man at the corner shop (whom I then thought was at least a hundred years old) what the people before the present residents there were called.

'The bloke was Peter Murray. I knew him well.'

I asked if Mr Murray had had any children. 'Oh four... well, one died young... Samuel.... A lung problem I recall.'

Theatre Royal, Bradford

Sir Henry Irving (1838-1905) is indeed one of the great names in the history of the English theatre; he was the first actor to be knighted, and all accounts of him agree that his performances were magnetic and made compulsive viewing. More recently, we have had new insights into his touring as scholars have researched the life of Bram Stoker, creator of *Dracula*, who was Irving's assistant for many years.

It has long been on record that Irving's ghost haunts the Theatre Royal in Bradford. He collapsed in the foyer of the Midland Hotel while staying in Bradford as his company was presenting *Becket*. As Peter Underwood comments, it was a fitting place for his ghost to appear, such was his love of his art.

Mixenden Highwayman

Between Mixenden Reservoir and the Keighley road near Halifax, stands Fold Farm. Although modernity has encroached a little on these few square miles of crags and pasture, and there are some computer companies not far away now, it is easy to imagine what the place must have been like in the eighteenth century.

Fold Farm has a powerful supernatural narrative attached to its history, and there is no doubt which event was the most striking and dramatic. There are slightly different versions of what happened there that gave rise to the farm's own spectre, and the first was told me by Eileen Nichols. One day a serving maid opened the door to see a young man on the doorstep, clearly faint and weak, in need of food and drink. He asked to be let in, and, perhaps against her better judgement in the wild times of the 1750s, she did so.

As the man sat down and they talked, she noticed that he had a pistol at his hip. The poor girl panicked; she was making him some good, warm food, and decided that the safest action was to strike first. These were tough times, and without a police force, you struck first and asked questions later. The poor girl threw a pan of hot water over the man and fled. He managed to over-ride the pain it seems, and followed her in a rage. He caught her and murdered her. The young woman's unhappy spirit walks the farm at certain times.

Another version is that the highwayman was in fact scalded badly by a pan of fat, and that in fact he had entered dressed in woman's clothes, and that the maid had seen his hairy arm while she was cooking. It was a ruse that would have been used by the robbers and footpads of those years. Some say that the robber was in fact the notorious James Hey, a villain who had a rough gang of footpads in the Huddersfield and Halifax area – but they were out and about in slightly later times.

John Nichols is sure that the disguise ruse was the real tale here; what is interesting is that ghost stories are often narratives that overlap with folklore, and there are almost infinite variations on the 'disguised robber' story. Clearly, there is some substance underneath all this. One thing is for sure: the farm was situated in such an isolated spot at that time that its family would have been vulnerable to the highwaymen around, eager to exploit the people who were well away from their neighbours.

Sir John Hotham's Ghost in Beverley

This is a ghost story from the dark years of the English Civil War when brother fought against brother. The central figure is Sir John Hotham, who was the governor of Hull in 1642 when King Charles I and his army came to the city and insisted that the gates of Hull be opened to him. Hotham did not open the gates. The king wanted the magazine (the arsenal) in Hull Castle, of course. It was important to him.

He had disobeyed his king and when the city was entered, Charles wanted revenge on Hotham and ordered his troops to throw the man over the city walls to his death, but again they ignored this, and eventually Hotham took his own followers to Beverley. He was a man with an interesting life – having had five wives and also finding time to be M.P. for Beverley. It was at the Old White Hart Inn in Hull that Hotham and friends voted not to allow Charles into the city.

Naturally, Hotham was thought of as a traitor for his actions against his sovereign and he was arrested. He had run off to Scarborough but was caught and it was while he was being brought through Beverley by the market place, he tried to escape by dashing up an alley. But poor Hotham was seized after being

The Guildhall, Beverley. Many inexplicable events have been linked to this, and Hotham passed by before his violent death.

slammed by a musket butt. That spot would be a place of misery ever after: he knew his days were numbered, and it was in Beverley at that moment that he knew there was just one route open for him – to the scaffold.

Lady Hotham worked hard to try to gain a pardon for her husband but Hotham was court martialled at the London Guildhall, and there was high drama indeed when we note that his own son (who was a lawyer) was given the task of defending his father. The son failed, and the scaffold waited for Sir John Hotham. He told the world that he was innocent of treason and then he placed his head on the block at the Tower. His brother took the head and body and put them in a coffin.

But that dark, narrow lane in Beverley has been somehow tainted and cursed ever since. Some have said that, walking alone there, they sense an overwhelming feeling of despair. Reports have been given swearing that horses have been heard there, followed by a yell of pain, and yet there is nothing corporeal to be seen: it is merely that place of pain, a lane by the market in that beautiful town, forever destined to be a few yards in which a man's dark and agonising destiny of execution was felt to be certain.

Not only did Hotham die that day in London, but his son also: both were regarded as traitors in that dangerous time. Some say that the events in Hull were the beginning of that awful conflict that tore apart England and its people for six years.

York Museum Ghost

In 1953, the caretaker of the Yorkshire Museum in York, Mr Jonas, saw what he thought was a ghost – a little man who seemed to be from the Edwardian period. Mr Jones and his wife had locked up for the day and gone down to their basement room when they heard footsteps in the room above them. When the caretaker went upstairs, he saw a man, a person he thought at first was alive and substantial, seeming to be to him like an eccentric professor type. Mr Jonas told the paper what he saw, ' I saw an elderly man crossing from Mr Willmott's office into another room… When I got to the door he seemed to change his mind again and turned quickly to come out.'

The caretaker watched and followed the strange visitor, noting that he was wearing elastic-sided boots; he said that the big black buttons on the side of the man's coat looked 'old-fashioned.' Mr Jonas had had enough and he put out his hand to touch the man on the shoulder. However, as Mr Jonas told *the Yorkshire Post*: 'But as my hand drew near his coat he vanished and the book he had been holding dropped to the floor.'

That was only the beginning, because that book was to be significant in the period following that extraordinary vision. It was called *Antiquities and Curiosities of the Church*. About a month after the first sighting, when Mr Jonas had tried to get Mr Willmott, the curator, to be with him to corroborate any sightings, he was on his own when he saw the apparition again. But so urgent had the situation become that Mr Jonas had to have someone with him, knowing he had to show that it was not just his imagination; a man called Walter French joined him and they struck lucky, if that is the right way to put it: both men heard a noise and moved quickly to the location of that sound, and there on the floor was that book again, the pages still turning.

As it was becoming obvious that there was a pattern – visitations at twenty to eight on every fourth Sunday, Jonas gathered some allies and a group of seven men waited on the next date when it was expected that the old man would appear again. They were not disappointed with regard to the puzzling book. Sure enough, a book was seen in flight – and not by Mr Jonas himself but by his brother James, so there was some corroboration this time. There was that same book, on the floor again. James Jonas said that it had not fallen, not in the way we might think of a book falling from a shelf. The witness said it did not even fall at the same speed that a book would usually fall.

But matters escalated after that. The story became widely known, and naturally, some professional investigators arrived: they were Dingwall and Hall of the Society for Psychical Research, and unfortunately they were not convinced. They saw and heard nothing at their vigil, and the conclusion was that Mr Jonas had imagined it all. There was even an opinion expressed that the book had been moved through trickery – a wire used by some practical joker.

Piers Gaveston in Scarborough

Piers Gaveston, who was born in 1284, was the son of a Gascon knight who became the court favourite of King Edward II; they were very close and may well have had a homosexual relationship, as playwright

The ghosts of York are now the subject of a 'ghost walk'.

Christopher Marlowe depicted the story in his play, *Edward II*. But whatever the real nature of their friendship, when Edward began to give Gaveston all kinds of valuable gifts (including the earldom of Cornwall) Gaveston was pressured into going into a life of exile and disgrace in 1309. After a struggle and all kinds of ploys to try to survive over the next few years, he surrendered at Scarborough. He had caused all kinds of trouble. As one writer of the time put it: 'Gaveston had by his insolence so exasperated the barons of England that they entered into a confederacy for the purpose of expelling him from the kingdom.'

The Merchant Venturer's Hall, York.
Another place, close to the Museum, with its own grounded spirits.

The old chapel in the grounds of Scarborough Castle.

Edward had made Gaveston the governor of Scarborough Castle and he was left there, perhaps in a situation that might have been considered safe, given the impressive defences of that mighty edifice. But the earls Pembroke, Warren and de Percy laid siege to Scarborough and, through lack of food, Gaveston gave in. Although the lords swore an oath that they would not harm him, it meant nothing and he was beheaded at Blacklow Hill in Warwickshire in 1312.

Edward took revenge on Scarborough, installing some ruthless governors there, but the real survival appears to be Gaveston's unruly and restless spirit. The castle is a dour, tough place: the fortifications are overpowering, and in the centre there is the chapel dug into the earth: all centuries are represented in that powerful stonework brooding over the North Sea. Among the slopes and battlements there still appears to be Piers Gaveston – and without his head, some say.

He has been seen at the barbican gate, by the east wall and most commonly close to where there was once an Angoo-Saxon chapel. Some say that the old chapel is where the spectre tends to be most often sensed, as if his tormented soul is seeking some religious consolation. Whatever the truth, his story is a melancholy one: a man left alone and rejected, weak and easily overcome in those warlike times when the hardest men came out winners.

The Dog Ornament Exorcism

The doyen of ghost-hunters, Peter Underwood, met one of Yorkshire's most busy and successful exorcists when working on his book on haunted places in 1996. This was no less a person that the Archbishop of York's adviser on paranormal events and experiences, the Rev. Tom Willis. Tom spoke to Underwood about one of his strangest poltergeist cases: an exorcism in Hull.

Willis went to the house and sat down with the people in the house and also with a police officer. He noticed that there were some objects on the mantelpiece: a clock, an ashtray, a candlestick, a kettle and a little ornament of a toy dog. Then the dog ornament just disappeared, and someone drew the assembled group's attention to that fact. Willis was amazed to hear movement and sounds coming from the adjoining kitchen. As they walked through, the ornament was on the floor. Willis told Underwood, ' For a moment I thought someone was playing a joke and had come in through the back door with a replica, but the only outside door was locked and on the inside.'

This case is one of a remarkable number of such paranormal events in which objects are moved from place to place. Poltergeist activity is still something which baffles us, giving rise to innumerable theories. But moving objects are a source of intrigue. There have been many reports of such things, and in a house in Halifax I have seen such a phenomenon with my own eyes. A school bag lying on a high shelf suddenly flew across a kitchen in a plain terrace house, landing on the floor by the sleeping dog of the family. 'It does that a lot' my correspondent told me. 'It always seems to be thrown at the poor dog!'

But the exorcist in Hull was in no doubt that the restless spirit was at work and needed to be put to peaceful inactivity. As an adviser on paranormal events, Willis had to have an open mind on these matters, and try to do whatever 'worked' even if the explanations will perhaps never be known.

The Scarcroft Case

The peaceful stretch of land north of Leeds, towards Wetherby, contains a cluster of beautiful villages lying in farming country. Although these places are just a few miles from the A1 road north, it would not be wrong to call them idyllic. This is an area of old churches, well-kept gardens and open fields. But as well as the stories of old-time hunting, shooting and fishing, there is one long road, leading from Scarcroft into the country, which appears to be a place where a ghost is grounded – the ghost of a woman whose life was taken in her own home, back in 1948.

At that time, Ling Lane was a quiet place, and Ann Barker's cottage was in a quiet spot. As was often the practice in country places in those days, Ann Barker kept a shotgun, and she stored it in the eaves of the roof. Not long before Christmas, 1948 an intruder came into her home and battered her to death.

She was found lying on the floor near her front door; she had lived a quiet life, and kept herself to herself. But there is nothing quiet about her spirit. Some say she walks that long road in the deep winter, trying to tell people about her killer, because the fact is that the person who took her life was never found. A deliveryman was walking on the road from his van one evening, a parcel in his hands, when he felt that he was being watched. He looked up the lane and saw an old woman staring at him, then waving for him to come to her. 'She was white-haired, thin... seemed to have a fur coat on.' At first he thought she was real – a substantial figure who maybe thought he had a delivery for her. But when he shouted a reply, saying he was busy and could she wait a minute, she faded away. 'She seemed to turn and walk, then she was a blur.'

There was a theory at the time that some migrant workers around the area might have been involved in the deed, but nothing was proved. Not only do we have an unsolved murder: we have an unhappy ghost in that tree-lined, peaceful place.

Burton Agnes

In 1965, Harry Scott wrote about Burton Agnes hall in this way: 'a lovely Elizabethan house of red brick and stone dressings, with graceful bow windows in the projecting wings framing the recessed central portion of the front... It welcomes you in a courtly manner as a gracious dowager might…' Much earlier, the traveller, Celia Fiennes wrote: ' It looks finely in the approach.' These writers were also aware of the other side of matters there. It may be just a legend, but it is a harrowing tale for all that.

The story is about Anne, one of the daughters of Sir Henry Griffith. She loved the house, and she was always looking at the work being done, seeing its beauty shaped and crafted. She would want to be in no other place; but one day she was sent on an errand to Harpham and on her way back home, the poor girl was attacked and left for dead on the road. She was carried home, mortally ill; Anne begged her sisters that, whatever might happen in the future, her skull was to stay in the house she loved so much. She vowed that, if ever it was to be taken away, she would haunt the house.

Her body was, of course, buried outside, and what happened then seemed to fulfil the prophecy: there were noises in the house and all the signs of what we today would call poltergeist activity. Tables were knocked over; windows slammed, and nobody could have any rest in the place. There was nothing else to do but bring the skull back into the house. But in 1867, a young maid was spring cleaning at the hall and she opened an old cupboard. In there she found the skull, but she knew nothing of the story behind it. The maid picked up the skull, using a knitting needle through the eye socket because she didn't have the nerve to pick it up, and she threw the skull out of the window onto a pile of manure.

The horse pulling the cart was suddenly excited and very restless and nothing could move the beast. An old maid, when she was told that the skull had been thrown out of the hall, yelled a command for it to be taken inside again. The old lady told the young maid the tale of the spirit the staff knew as 'Old Nance.'

Middleham Music and Pontefract Murders

There are many castles in Yorkshire, and most can lay claim to having ghostly inhabitants, but few can rival these two gaunt places for such reputations.

Middleham Castle was built by Robert Fitzrandolph from around 1170, after being a stronghold in the possession of William the Conqueror's nephew, Alan Rufus from 1069. It was where Richard III spent much of his childhood and has always had strong Ricardian connexions – and for that reason it is dear to the hearts of Yorkshiremen. The Tudors simply let the place rot, and so we have to imagine the daunting grandeur of the stronghold, with its portcullis and massive wooden gates.

It was clearly a considerably important place at the time of the Wars of the Roses, but now its clamour of battle is just one of the many ghostly sounds associated with it. One of the most common experiences is that people have reported hearing the soothing music of the medieval period; but there have been accounts of the sounds of battle being heard outside the walls. Children on one occasion said that they had seen a knight galloping. Of course, in this age of re-enactments of battles and skirmishes, we can never be sure of these things in military installations, but in Middleham the tales have been so common that there is surely some foundation here worth investigating.

Pontefract is such a focus for paranormal activity that the castle has a regular ghost walk. The atmosphere is forbidding and packed with resonances from some of the bloodiest conflicts of English history, and also includes in its grim chronicle of pain the murder of a king – Richard II – that event being a scene in Shakespeare's play of that name.

After the horrendously savage and long Battle of Towton on Palm Sunday, 1461, Lord Salisbury was taken prisoner and holed up in Pontefract. There he was executed, and his head was to be put on the Micklegate Bar in York with a paper crown place on it. There is no wonder then, in the belief that the aristocrat's pained and restless spirit walks the castle.

As for Richard II, he was killed there, and Shakespeare gives him some final words which express his hope of heaven:

> 'That hand shall burn in never-quenching fire
> That staggers thus my person. Exton, thy fierce hand
> Hath with the king's blood stained the king's own land.
> Mount, mount my soul! Thy seat is up on high...'

But could it be that the king's soul never did reach 'on high'? Does it wander around the place of death, in torment? Many think that is the case, and this crime scene is one that arguably has that voice of pain moaning in its dark places, as if the king was tormented in hell, not his killer.

The ghost walk tells the tale, and anyone bold enough to venture in there should expect the earl or the king to be there, sad spirits who were never given the grace of a dignified death by their enemies.

Hellen-Pot Boggart

The Victorian writer and clergyman Sabine Baring-Gould, best known for his hymn, *Onward Christian Soldiers*, was also a great researcher into things paranormal, and he told the tale of the boggart of Hellen-Pot. He once walked with his friend, Mr Keene, out to Arncliffe and beyond. He recalled that they walked beyond that place, up a track, and had a feeling that he had 'left civilisation entirely behind ' him.

Like so many amateur scientists of his age, Baring-Gould was keen on hunting for rocks and fossils and he had his collection-bag with him; he became so preoccupied with that work that he lost track of where he was, and then night fell.

One of the most frightening experiences of the Yorkshire moors in that area is stepping into a 'pot' – a well, very common in the limestone topography. He had split from his friend and was alone when, in the dark, he was aware that someone was walking rapidly behind him. He wrote:

'His walk was strange, a wriggle and duck accompanying each step,
The reason being, as I ascertained when he came alongside of me,
That he was a cripple in both legs.'

When the writer commented that it was a dark night, the voice spoke: 'Darker, darker below.'

We can imagine Baring-Gould's feelings then. He found the courage to ask the way to Arncliffe. But the being walked on ahead and gave no answer. The writer shouted now, several times, trying to get the thing's attention, but he walked on. But then he heard the splash of something in a beck a little way in front of him, and saw the figure go down into the water. He then sensed a lantern light in front of him, and he could make out the face of a young woman; then something seemed to grasp him, and at that moment came the worst horror – he saw the man 'sink down the abyss with the light reflected from his upturned face.'

The writer was desperate: he had to go to the nearest farmhouse and beg for shelter for the night. It was there, when he had been given a glass of ale, that the farmer said, 'It's the boggart lass, he's taken to misleading folk again!'

The farmer told the exhausted Baring-Gould that the boggart was supposed to grab people and tug them down into the earth. The story was that around the middle of the eighteenth century, a foreigner came to the locality and married a local girl; but he was arrested for bigamy and taken away, and the young wife pined for him. She wandered on the moors looking for him, but in vain. The officers who came for him had said that he escaped and ran out into the moors, so the girl looked for him, again and again, but the theory was that he had gone down into one of the pots and died down there.

Baring-Gould was not lacking in courage. He went back again to the little farm with his friend Keene, and they took ropes with them. He went down, and as he entered the darkness, he said that 'in one second I saw the face of the boggart flash up at me full of hideous triumph and I felt the grip of his arms about my waist. Next moment I lost all consciousness.'

He awoke to find Keene and the farmer bending over him, and amazingly, he was well again, and walked back to Arncliffe, stunned. His friend Keene forcibly let him know how worried he had been that he would never see his friend again.

Baring-Gould has to be one of the most fearless and intrepid paranormal investigators on record. Of course, there is nothing to suggest that the boggart was removed from the pot. He may be there, if anyone were to walk on that track beyond Arncliffe today.

SHUDDERS AND SHADOWS
MY OWN ENCOUNTERS
WITH GHOSTS

The serious parapsychologists, trying hard to be properly scientific and rational when they enquire into paranormal accounts by individuals, insist on such experience being replicated. In other words, that walk in the dark you had five years ago – it needs to be reproduced before it might be taken seriously by science. They would have you choose a similar night, at the same time of year, and then have you walk the same route, and as far as possible in the same frame of mind. This is, of course, ludicrous.

The tales recounted here may not all have such potential, but there are some stories rather similar to that of Nigger, the labrador of Wing Commander Guy Gibson, who led the Dam Busters from Scampton in Lincolnshire. Nigger sits at the gate, or is seen around the entrance, on the same July evening every year. That is as close as we might come to repeated manifestations in this area of activity. A neighbour of mine swore that his cat came back every Christmas, always and only then, its shape seen as the man sat in the kitchen, and a rub against his legs as he was cooking.

But generally, these tales (and the legends alongside) are embedded in that inescapable consciousness of *ourselves*: the condition we have, being in the bubble of ourselves. So, when we feel sure that something or someone has breathed on our neck while walking upstairs, only that specific person – that network of those specific nerves – felt that sensation. The belief is therefore 'unscientific' but try telling that to someone who lives every day with a 'cold spot' in their home, or footsteps treading across the bedroom floor above them. These are very common experiences.

Here are some cases from my own case book. In these, I have actually witnessed inexplicable events.

Harry Returns

I had a phone call from a woman I knew who lived in a village just a few miles from Seacroft in north Leeds. She said that I ought to come and see what her house spirit was up to. Apparently it was in the habit of moving a carriage clock and sitting in a favourite chair.

'The worst thing is,' Mrs M said when I arrived, 'he used to dig in a vegetable garden just round the side, but now that patch is gone, and he raps on the window if there's a sunny day.'

I asked what she meant.

'Well, it's Harry, he used to dig there, he grew leeks and peas. He used to bang on the window. It's the ghost of Harry, my husband, I know it is.'

I arrived one June morning and stood outside to take in the location. It was a large bungalow on the corner of a crescent; the houses around had been there since about 1930 I would say. In Mrs M's home there was a broad lawn by the gate and a large flower garden to one side. That was what had become of the vegetable plot.

'The worst thing is... well, like last week, I went out to the local shops. It would be about ten in the morning. I was out for about an hour, and when I got back, I stooped to open the gate and I had to put my bags down. As I glanced up towards the house I could see something through the glass door. It was like a dark shape, an outline of something.'

Mrs M was nervous as she walked slowly up the drive, wondering if she had an intruder. There is a lot of robbery in her area, even in the day. A few of her neighbours had had kids break in and steal electrical appliances and small possessions.

'I wondered whether to call Hilary from Number 8. She's my pal really. But I walked on and looked into the kitchen through the window. My heart nearly stopped there and then. I mean Harry died four years ago, and there he was, sitting at the kitchen table, like he always did. He always used to wait for me to make him his morning tea – never did it himself!'

She dropped the shopping and recalled that a shiver went through her. For a few seconds she froze. Then Harry just went away in a 'sort of misty way' Mrs M said.

She opened the door and rushed inside then. But there was nobody. She said that the figure had been wearing a brown pullover and a white shirt and wore thick-rimmed glasses – all just as Harry would have worn.

'It's happened just the once. But the knocks on the window can be every day for a few weeks, depending on the weather!' She said.

Hilary arrived and the three of us had some tea. The two women told me all about the objects moving in that room. I sensed that I was being told certain things, and I said, without thinking, 'Harry had a dog – a little brown one.' They looked at me, astonished. 'I don't know why I said that..'

'No, but you're right.'

It was then that I realised that in a little lean-to around the back, there was a strange sound, like a slapping and tapping noise. I asked what it could be but neither had heard it. We stood up and walked towards the lean-to. A plant-pot fell on the concrete and cracked.

'Harry used to do his tomato plants in there. Oh God, he's here now isn't he?'

Well it was nothing to be afraid of. I said all the obvious things to placate the widow. Mrs M had become accustomed to her late husband's visits. But still there were surprises, and I had been fortunate enough to be there when one of these occurred.

The Grey Lady at the Cottages

I responded to a call to go out into a village where my friend Jean had said one of her neighbours was having early morning visits from a woman – but she was not alive!

Imagine a row of small cottages, very old, still surviving in the midst of a newly-created estate of commuter homes. This was one little street with a tiny, disused Methodist church at one end and three small two-up two-down homes, places with a history going back to around 1750.

I went to the house where the reports had come from. Mr S told me that it had happened several times: he or his wife had got up in the early hours to go to the toilet upstairs and seen a young woman walk along the tiny corridor between rooms, then apparently merge into a wall.

I went upstairs to look around. There were the two small rooms, and the miniscule bathroom opposite one of them. The landing across this area was only perhaps twelve feet long before it ended in the old wall of the adjoining property.

'How about next door?' I asked. Surely they had seen the apparition too. I was told that was exactly right. The neighbours had seen her too, and at more or less the same time.

I said that I would try to find out something about the house; there was a fair amount of history available and documents had been kept. I looked around in the nearest library and had the most amazing stroke of luck – there was an old almanac and a cuttings book. There it was, a strange reference in an old newspaper cutting from around 1920 – a piece telling the tale of Mary Cooper, a girl who took her own life, put alongside a piece from the almanac telling the story, and of course, suicide was a crime in 1920. The poor girl had committed a serious offence.

I told the family, 'It looks like it was a case of unrequited love... Mary's young man went to live and work across the seas,' I said.

'Well, she can stay... we don't want no exorcist!' Mr S said, with a smile.

A Guardian Spirit?

There has always been a belief that we have a spirit who watches over us; the ancient Greeks believed in this *daemon*. Charles had one for sure. He asked me to listen to his story one day when I was enjoying a Sunday drink in the sun. There he sat, an accountant (supposedly down to earth and full of good sense) telling me that one day, as he had sat in just such a place and on a Sunday, he had heard a voice say, 'Go and get another pint, Charles.' He said he had done so, and only later did he realise that he had walked to the bar in a kind of trance.

But as he had stood at the bar, there had been an almighty crash from the yard outside. There were screams and people scrambled inside, yelling in fear.

In the beer garden outside there was a delivery van lying across the table where Charles had been sitting. The driver had slammed his head and been concussed, but survived. Luckily, no-one was near that table, though many were close and ran off in abject terror when the van careered from the road into the garden. It had ploughed through a low privet hedge, gone at the table where Charles had been and cracked into the wall behind.

Lindholme Willie

What is today a massive prison, H M P Lindholme near Doncaster, was once a base for the R A F. A bomb on show outside the prison administration office commemorates its former identity. The site is vast, with green-painted buildings still surviving from the R A F days. There remains the huge parade ground in the centre and a massive hangar, rotting inside, standing by the old control tower on the prison boundary. On 18 August, 1940, the airfield changed from Hatfield Woodhouse to Lindholme, and it closed as an airfield in 1970.

Spirits from the next world have often been heard on the staircase between what is now the library and some offices. Those areas in wartime were the NAAFI and the room where the fighter crews would spend time before their high-risk flights into the deathly skies.

The area of the prison extends a long way, but beyond that there is Lindholme waste land, reaching into the bogs of the Isle of Axholme. Centuries ago, the hermit of what was then an island was the most celebrated character around the place, but since the war with Hitler, another person has dominated the Lindholme story, a figure often seen around the camp and the village of nearby Hatfield Woodhouse. But he is not alive and in this world.

This is Lindholme Willie, sometimes 'Billy', a man in pilot's gear who has been seen from time to time by all kinds of people. Our story begins with an excavation in the marsh. In the *Doncaster Advertiser* for 30 July, 1967, we have this report:

H M P Lindholme, where the pained ghost of Lindholme Willie roams.

'Fighter Pilot's Body Found
Forensic experts are trying to unravel the mystery surrounding
the body of a Polish airman who died in the last war.
The well-preserved body was recovered from a peat bog on
Hatfield Moor near Doncaster by a peat cutter. It has no dog-tags
and was not in an aircraft – though the uniform he was wearing
was preserved in the peat.
Now forensic and R A F experts are trying to discover how the
body came to rest in the peat – which also houses several crashed
aircraft, including a Lancaster bomber.'

The body was about nine feet down in the peat when found, just a mile into the heath from H M P Lindholme. A spokesman at the time said he believed it was the body of a Polish airman who fought with the freedom fighters against Germany. But that was all they did know. The remains were given a full military burial.

The stories about encounters with Lindholme Willie are many; several people say that they have been approached by an airman with jacket and hat, rather bedraggled, and asking for directions to the Operations Room, or sometimes asking for the health care quarters. Apparently, before he gets his answer he has vanished.

In a forum discussion people wrote to say that he had been seen standing outside the Bay Horse public house in Hatfield. One correspondent had a memory from the 1960s when he lived in Dunscroft; he said he was told by his mother about Lindholme Willie – and that was when his body had just been found, so it hints at some of the first sightings. That writer suggests that the long and uneasy history of Hatfield Chase and Lindholme was well known when he was young, and that Ash Hill and Hatfield church were always 'full of mystery' – he notes that a

Guests at the Bay Horse, Hatfield,
have seen Willie near here.

secret tunnel from the moors to the church was found at one time, a place where local monks could hide from the Danish invaders.

As to Willie, there have been theories as to which plane he was in when he crashed. We know that Polish squadrons 304 and 305, with Wellington bombers, were based at Lindholme in the years 1941-42, but most likely lines of thought lead to planes from other squadrons that came down. The most probable is a Wellington, number W5557 SM-G that came down on the way home from a bombing operation on Cologne. It came onto Hatfield Moor, killed three civilians, and on board were three Poles who died: Sergeant Leyche, Sergeant Wasilenko and Sergeant Buszko.

But whoever he was, Willie persists and will not go away. In recent years, prison staff have given reports of a figure on the stairs in the Leger Building. Ghosts are often seen on stairways and steps, or in lanes and alleys, places where there is a potential transit from one state of being to another. At Lindholme, he has been seen walking down the stairs, and some have heard a voice ask a question as they walk through into some staff toilets at the foot of the stairs: the voice usually asks, 'I need some help, can you put this right? Or 'Madam, I need some help here, quick.'

One witness to Willie's appearance told me that he was working late one evening in October and walked across the parade-ground. As he was near the centre he was aware of someone watching him. 'I had that tingling in the neck, you know...' he said. When he turned around, thinking he would see a fellow officer, he saw a man in leathers, holding something that looked like a heavy bag in one hand. The figure grimaced in pain, held out a hand, and then faded into the evening half-light.

Officers on night duty have heard band music coming from what is now a large office. One man told me that he once had to find somewhere to sleep, so he had a mattress on a landing, and as he lay there, he heard music from the long room next door. When he nervously went through the double gate to have a look, he switched the light on and there was no-one there.

It looks as though Lindholme Willie will go on disturbing people, and not only within the prison. He has been seen on the roads around the village and he may be there outside the Bay Horse at any time, asking where he can find a doctor.

As to my own experience, while working in H M P Lindholme, as a writer, I can say that I had one experience which I can only explain with reference to the unquiet soul of Willie. I was walking near a boundary, not far from the old control tower (which is outside the gaol); my eyes told me that a man was standing by the high fence, watching me, and I closed my eyes and rubbed them. I then looked again; he waved as if trying to catch my attention, and then he started walking towards me. I thought he was a member of staff, but he was not wearing dark-coloured clothes. As he came nearer, it seemed that I could only see his top half and the legs were suddenly blurred. Then he went from sight entirely.

Was it Lindholme Willie? I like to think so.

The Arrival of 'Jimmy'

Near Doncaster, in a plain everyday semi-detached (address not to be given) Jimmy arrived one day. He was not a relative or a school friend. He was not a neighbour, but the house was in a cemetery road, and that later was to be important. The boy in the house, just six years old, started telling his parents about his friend Jimmy. That's not uncommon, as mum and dad knew that children have 'imaginary friends' but this became so frequent that they began to think it was not healthy.

'Mam, Jimmy says he's going to burn the shed down!' was one worrying statement at breakfast. Then at another time, he said, 'Jimmy was cutting his hair with your big kitchen knife...'

Should they take the boy to see a doctor? A shrink maybe? After a few months, when they were about to make a decision on that, the boy walked in, clearly upset, and said, 'Mam... Jimmy's hanging at the top of the stairs!'

After that, there was no more talk of Jimmy. But one day when the boy was a little older, he came in from school and tugged at his mother's arm. 'You have to come... you have to come, now mam!'

He led her, unwillingly, out into the street and then several hundred yards to the massive wrought-iron gated entrance to the cemetery.

'What is it son?' She shouted.

'See that grave stone? The Kerrigan family... buried here.'

'So, I don't understand.'

'Mam, Jimmy was called Kerrigan – but he's not here. I've looked all over the graveyard. There are no other Kerrigans.

There were Thomas, Elizabeth, Albert and George. No James.

His mother explained about suicides not being buried in sacred ground. 'Maybe that's the reason' she said. The boy brooded for a few days and then he made his own cross, with 'Jimmy' on a piece of cardboard on it. He put it in a corner of the grave yard on the way to school, and he felt better about it.

His mother told me, 'It didn't matter that it would be taken away. He just knew he did the right thing!'

The Restaurant Visitor

I was asked to give my opinion about certain unexplained happenings at the garden centre restaurant. One week there had been some aprons removed. 'The pinnies disappeared!' my friend said. 'One minute they were there and then, gone!' The staff looked everywhere but with no success. Then there were gloves vanishing into nowhere and something or someone was locking cupboard doors and the keys were on the hook at the back of the room.

That all seemed harmless, though unnerving. Then one day my friend said, 'Oh God, this week it's been blood-stained gloves in a cupboard.'

She explained that a part-time worker had opened a cupboard door to get some gloves and jumped with shock as she saw the oven-gloves stained with what seemed to be fresh blood. The first thought was that someone preparing meat must have used them, but it was before the shift started that the gloves were found.

The manager explored the possibility of a practical joker being on the staff, but all eight workers were long-serving, reliable and well known. None of them had a track record of that kind of dark humour. Then, although it seems bizarre, one day a woman who had worked there longer than anyone else, after finding her coat on the floor outside the kitchen rather than on the hook, said, ' Oh for Christ's sake, get lost and leave us alone!'

The 'thing' did indeed. There was no disturbance after that sharp request. The tenseness turned to fun as the staff all told her she should be a medium. 'Yes you've got something there, Evelyn... a sixth sense' they said. But there were no more visitations after that piece of bravado.

Unexplained Noises in a Ghost Towns Experience

While taking part in *Derek Acorah's Ghost Towns* television programme as historical adviser a few years ago, I was staying at a hotel near Halifax. It was a snowy January and there was that eerie silence we feel when snow somehow insulates much of the normal sounds around. It was a

Sunday and I went for a walk around the parish church.

I had stopped for a few seconds in the evening twilight, close to the church walls, and I was aware of shuffling sounds from around the corner. It sounded like an animal – the kind of noise dogs might make if snuffling or digging. I walked slowly around to where the noise was coming from, but there was nothing to see – and yet I could still hear the sounds, as if there was something just a few feet from me.

After that I tried to look into the history and ask around to see if anyone had had similar experiences, but there was nothing. But I recall Derek Acorah talking about things he calls 'elementals' and somehow his description made sense.

I didn't mention it on the programme.

Oakwood Lane Again

Of all the places in the Leeds suburbs where there are paranormal activities in abundance, Oakwood Lane has to be one of the most 'alive with the dead.' I determined to spend some time there late at night after so many people had reported seeing a woman in white walking there around midnight. I thought that the cliché of such a thing was ridiculous; that this was merely a case of over-active imaginations. But in 1968, after a late night at someone's house locally, I went along the lane to wait, out of sight of anyone, to watch, observe and take note. There had been at least three sightings by what is now an old building used for a very modern purpose, and it was a cold night. I remember stamping my feet and blowing into my hands. I have a vivid recollection of there being several winters then which were markedly colder than today.

Things became even worse; my teeth actually began to chatter with the cold. I know that my jaw felt as if it were about to seize up. I thought that this was an escapade for someone deranged, and started walking back home. As with so many investigations, things happened at the moment when I was 'switching off' from a vigilance watch. Ahead of me, as if walking out of a front-gate of an old villa, there was a shape of what seemed like a woman, wearing a fur garment; I lost all control and stupidly called out to her, saying, 'Who are you?'

It was an idiotic thing to do. It moved across the quiet lane as if being blown by a strong gust of wind, and I ran to the spot on the other side of the road to see if she had gone into another quiet lane that leads into

Oakwood Lane, a focus for visitors from beyond the grave.

Gipton woods. It seemed to go in that direction. I walked a little way, and heard noises in the trees – it would have been squirrels most likely.

The cold drove me back home into the warmth. I have been since, but at times when there was too much noise. This is a place, I'm sure, where a proper investigation needs to be set up.

The Reservoir Ghost

Seventy years ago, in the quiet village of Fewston between Skipton and Harrogate, there was a brutal murder of a housewife – an unsolved case. The woman was working in the village shop when someone came in and battered her to death; she lay in a pool of blood. The village was shocked. There was even more to lament, as there had been another murder there in which a car-dealer killed one of his rivals. It has been felt to be a place with a certain dark shadow over it, and the brooding waters of the Fewston Reservoir maybe contain some secrets.

The church at Fewston. Does a ghost tread here,
waiting for release to the next world?

The stories I came across were about a night-walker. People have seen a man walking slowly north towards the Swinsty Reservoir, taking a quiet, little-known back path. The figure hums a tune as he walks, and people have said hello to him, only to be ignored. Is he real and substantial?

The place has ancient stories, going back to the days of witchcraft, and some say that there is a focus for spirits in search of rest after a violent death. One young man taking his dog down there reported meeting the walker, and in daylight. He said that the shape appeared to take a roundabout route, to avoid coming close, and as he glanced around, the figure had gone, but the dog knew something was wrong. He stared and barked aggressively.

It's a tranquil spot, but folk should be aware that they may meet a stranger who just doesn't want to talk.

Reasons for Unexplained Encounters

I hope that these stories have added to the subjective lists of testimony to the uncanny and the unexplained, even if they may not be scientific. The nature of the subject is such that something happens, the person is convinced that there is no rational explanation, and the tale is told. After that, with or without science, we have to accept something as given, and as responded to by an individual.

In the titles of these tales, maybe the word 'ginnels' has been most neglected. But it must be said that the ginnels and snickets of West Yorkshire are one of the most distinctively creepy and atmospheric features of the conurbations. There are also the courts – dark and dingy places, enclosed by high walls and with corners the sun never penetrates. If ever a Tyke's mind is going to be preoccupied by thoughts of the super-natural it is in one of these spots. The story from Churwell illustrates the eerie nature of the dark squares and folds of the textile towns.

If you are a sceptic, reading these words now, all I can say is, spend a night at Temple Newsam or camp out next to Wainhouse Folly, but take a friend with you. The limits of our rational faculties are soon found out when the time and place are full of those indefinable effects we label 'interesting' when we mean 'inexplicable.'

Why do I involve myself in these investigations? The first reason is that I have always felt the need to find answers and explanations to anything that puzzles me. Then there is the sheer fascination with how and why paranormal events can provoke us to reconsider human life and the various theories about that flimsy veil which separates life from something else.

Finally, these stories and case book reports do relate to other documented experience across the world by all kinds of people, professional and amateur, and the number of similarities we have from this stock of material tends to impress researchers like me, and spurs us on to find more stories, so that gradually a series of 'template tales' emerge, a series of paranormal events with similarities. That makes each one more significant, as new meetings and experiences happen – and they do keep on happening, in the most ordinary places like the office, the factory or the railway station. We expect them to happen in churches, grave yards and old buildings, but phenomena are potentially everywhere and at any time. The challenge is to find new ways of understanding.

It is always amazing to learn that so many experiences have been conducted in an atmosphere of chance, whimsicality and hopefulness. With television ghost-hunts being so common now, the trappings of science are available, but one thing the stories from the past teach us is that some of the most convincing evidence for apparitions from beyond the grave has been seen while passing, from the corner of the eye.

Ghost on Camera and other St Mary's Tales

I have left until the very last tale the ghostly goings-on around the beautiful church of St Mary's in Beverley. The tales go back a long way. The most established one is of a phantom coach that has been heard many times heading through the town, past the market and towards the church. Even in recent years the sound has been heard. Some want to link the 'bad vibes' around the church and the North Bar with Dick Turpin, as he was a customer just across the road from the church at the Beverley Arms.

St Mary's, Beverley, where a ghost was caught on camera.

93

But most memorable of all has to be the time when the good folk of Yorkshire sat down to tea, around ten years ago, and saw a camcorder film of what looked like a spirit of a woman walking along a narrow corridor and then entering a room.

Most visitors to the church are told about the connection with Lewis Carroll, because in the chapel of St Michael in the chancel aisle is a carving which is of a rabbit walking straight and carrying a satchel, with the staff of a walking pilgrim. It is almost certain that Carroll (Charles Dodgson) came to Beverley. We know that his artist, Tenniel, searched high and low across the land for a model to base the rabbit drawing on.

That steals the limelight, but it has not often been recalled that St Mary's has had one of the very best and most convincing ghosts on camera we have in the records.

Categories?

My investigations have led me to feel that there are certain groupings of what we think of as 'ghostly experiences.' I think of them as (a) mood and suggestion (b) uncanny and (c) visitants

In terms of mood and suggestion, the most common is when we know the history, the typology of the manifestation that is supposed to link to a specific place. Typical of that is the spectre on the stairs so often recorded by people who are in bereavement. By 'uncanny' I mean something than has an aspect of knowledge required that human beings cannot possess. Typical of that is the idea of the 'elemental' – a type of spirit that even the best mediums tend to be worried by. These are beings which present an atmosphere of fear and panic, often giving sensual evidence of their presence. Visitants to a place are those spirits we tend to find who have a link to a place but are supposedly interred elsewhere, or dead but their resting-place is unknown.

Of all these, my own personal quest is to collect and try to understand as many of the second category as possible. When Derek Acorah and the *Most Haunted* team visited the Pendle witch country, it was the presence of 'elementals' that most upset the professional ghost-hunters present.

BIBLIOGRAPHY

Books

The books were particularly useful in adding to the research done for this book:

Anon. *True Ghost Stories of the British Isles* (Bounty Books, 2005)
Banks, William Stott, *A List of Provincial Words in use at Wakefield*
 (Russell Smith and W R Hall, 1865)
Baring-Gould, S., *Yorkshire Oddities: Incidents and Strange Events*
 (1894) (Smith Settle, 1987)
Campbell, Marie, *Curious Tales of Old West Yorkshire* (Sigma, 1999)
Campbell, Marie, *Strange World of the Brontës* (Sigma, 2001)
Cooper J.J., *Brewer's Book of Myth and Legend* (Helicon, 1992)
Fairfax-Blakeborough, J. and R., *The Spirit of Yorkshire* (Batsford, 1954)
Hardo, Trutz, *Children who Have Lived Before* (C W Daniel, 2000)
Jones, Steve, *Yorkshire, The Sinister Side* (Wicked Publications 2004)
Kellett, Arnold, *Yorkshire Dictionary* (Smith Settle, 1994)
Kristen, Clive, *Local Ghost Trails* (Wharncliffe, 1998)
MacGregor, Alasdair Alpin, *The Ghost Book* (Robert Hale, 1955)
Owens, Andy, *Yorkshire Stories of the Supernatural*
 (Countryside Books, 1999)
Scruton, William, *Pen and Pencil Pictures of Old Bradford*
 (Smith Settle 1985)
Thornton, David, *Leeds, The Story of a City* (Fort, 2002)
Underwood, Peter, *Guide to Ghosts and Haunted Places* (Piatkus, 1996)
Walker, Harold, *This Little Town of Otley* (R & S Educational, 1995)
Wilson, Colin, *Mysteries* (Grafton, 1978)
Wilson, Colin, *Poltergeist!* (New English Library, 1981)
Wray, Michael, *Ghosts and Ghouls of the East Riding*
 (Caedmon Storytellers, 2004)
Yorkshire Legends Collected by the *Dalesman* (1969)

Periodicals

Dalesman
Dalesman Annual
Down Your Way magazine: articles by Rowland Cooper in issues 72 and 77
Milltown Memories: article by Peter Harvey in issue 5.   Issy Shannon, the
   editor, has gathered an excellent reference collection in this series.

Newspapers

Doncaster Advertiser
Epworth Bells
Halifax Courier
Huddersfield Examiner
Telegraph and Argus
Yorkshire Evening Post
Yorkshire Post

Other sources

Ministry of Defence, *Crashed Military Aircraft of Historical Interest: notes for
   guidance of recovery groups.* M.O.D. 1986